BELIEVE IN YOUR
DREAMS

*BOOK*LOGIX®
Alpharetta, Georgia

ISBN: 978-1-61005-203-0
Library of Congress Control Number: 2012910214

Printed in the United States of America

∞This paper meets the requirements of ANSI/NISO Z39.48-1992 (Permanence of Paper)

All Scripture quotations are taken from biblecentral.com (http://daily.bibleversecentral.com/2009/06/bible-verses-about-believe-part-1/)

BELIEVE IN YOUR
DREAMS

my spiritual journey

Rhonda Leiva

This book is dedicated to my mother, Betty Thacker, father, Howard Thacker, and grandparents, Lucille and William Jackson Sr.

CONTENTS

WATER

FIRE

FOREWORD

I had the privilege of first meeting Rhonda via my radio show, "Angels On Call," on Sirius Stars 102 in December of 2007. Since then and through many calls, conversations and physical meetings, I've come to realize through my own intuitive abilities, that Rhonda Leiva has—without a doubt in my mind's eye—been blessed with a super sensitive, natural intuitive gift!

I've personally witnessed, as have many, how her gift has grown throughout the years in leaps and bounds! I recommend that anyone and everyone who questions their intuition read Rhonda's book! I, for one, couldn't put it down!

- Mary Rose Occhino

Psychic Intuitive, Intuitive Explorer of Consciousness; Author, Awakened Instincts, Seven Keys to Enhance Every Aspect of Your Life; Star of Syfy's - *Mary Knows Best*; Radio show host - "Angels On Call" (formerly on Sirius Stars) & Blogtalkradio.com host of "Intuitive Nation with Mary O!"

ACKNOWLEDGEMENTS

I'd like to take this opportunity to thank some very special people in my life here on earth and in heaven.

I want to thank my loving husband Brian, and my children, Jason, Jessica, and Jordan; my brother and protector James White; my sister, Melissa Thacker; my mother-in-law, Diann Leiva; my precious granddaughter, Dakota; and all of my family members and special friends who love me unconditionally and urge me to follow my dreams and to be the person that I'm meant to be.

I want to thank my dear friend Mary Occhino for always being there for me and listening when I feel like I have the weight of the world on my shoulders.

Special thanks to my designer Sara Strish, my editors Jessica Parker and Caroline Donahue, and everyone else at BookLogix.

INTRODUCTION

J was born in Rome, Georgia, on July 31, 1957. My mother and father divorced when I was a baby. After my parents' divorce, we didn't see much of my father because he moved out of state. Shortly after my parents' divorce, my mother, brother, and I moved in with my grandparents. My grandparents had a three bedroom home with one bathroom. My mother's two brothers also still lived at home, so needless to say, the house was pretty crowded. My mother, brother, and I slept in the same bed, which worked out just fine. It didn't matter how crowded the house was, all that mattered was that we were all together as a family with more love than I can ever express with words. My grandparents played a big part in our lives and made up for us not having a father figure. When looking back on the years that we lived with our grandparents, all I think about and feel is LOVE!!!

A few years later, my mother married my stepfather Howard Thacker. My mother knew my stepfather for quite some time before she married him. I was two when my mother and stepfather got married, and my brother and I both grew to love him. He was a very generous and loving man. My stepfather made us feel loved, and we knew he would always be there to take care of us. I refer to my stepfather as "father" throughout this book.

When I was growing up, I was a very sensitive child and had a fear of being separated from my parents. I was always scared of the dark and never wanted to sleep in my bedroom because I always sensed and felt a presence in my room. I would always end up sleeping in my brother's bed with him because I felt safe and protected there.

At the early age of five, I realized that I was different from most kids my age. I could feel and sense things that most people couldn't pick up on. I started having reoccurring dreams about being in a war zone; tanks were going through my home, and the fear I felt in those dreams was unbearable because I knew my entire family had been killed. The reoccurring dreams were so vivid that they would always wake me up out of a sound sleep. I know this dream was from a past life, and that is why I never wanted to be separated from my family.

I remember my first day of school. I was absolutely terrified of being separated from my parents. My father had to pry me out of my mother's arms in order to take me to school. Once I got to the school, I cried uncontrollably and didn't want my father to leave me. Every day was like this for a long time. To this day, I remember how scared

I was to be left all alone at school. I know it's normal for children to be frightened on their first day of school, but I knew my fear had a deeper meaning than what most kids experienced. Most kids, after a couple of days, would get used to being separated from their parents, but not me. It would take me weeks.

When I was ten years old, I found out my mother was going to have a baby, and I was so excited. When I would go to the store, I would always buy baby rattlers and other little toys. I could hardly wait for the arrival of my brother or sister. When I woke up on Friday, October 13, 1967, I was elated because I knew my mother would give birth to my sister or brother that day. No one told me this was going to happen; I just woke up knowing it. Before leaving for school, I told my mother she was going to have the baby that day. When I came home from school later that evening, my mother was sitting on the couch looking at her watch, and I asked her what she was doing. She said, "I'm timing the labor pains to see how far apart they are to know when it is time to go to the hospital." I really didn't know anything about labor pains. I was just excited to meet my new baby brother or sister. A few minutes later, my mother asked me to call my father at work and tell him that he needed to get home because it was finally time to go to the hospital; she was about to have the baby. My father worked just up the street, so he was home in a matter of minutes. The next thing I knew, my father, mother, brother, and I were on the way to the hospital. My mother was in a lot of pain, so my father was going very fast, blowing the horn and flashing the car lights. I was terrified that he was going to lose control and wreck the car. When we arrived safely at the hospital, my mother was in even more pain, and my father rushed her into the hospital. It was just a matter of minutes until she had our baby sister, Melissa Irene Thacker. After the birth of my sister, we were all so happy.

A year after my sister was born, my mother and father started having marital problems and separated. After the separation, my mother, brother, sister, and I went back to live with my grandparents until my mother could get back on her feet. My brother and I were excited to go back and live with our grandparents, even though we were sad that our mother and father were no longer together. We loved our father and missed him very much. He promised to come and visit us as often as possible.

My family's religion was Church of Christ, so I was brought up being told that only God knew what was going to happen in the future, no one else. When I continued having dreams that would really happen I feared it was something evil from the Devil.

When I was young, I really didn't understand why I had dreams that often came true, or how I knew certain events would take place before they actually did. With a lack of understanding and a fear of evil lurking, I did not embrace my gift, rather feared it. After my mother's passing, I gained a better understanding of these dreams: what they meant, how to identify them, and what to pay attention to, which led me to the resolve that these dreams were a blessing, a true gift from God.

All of the dreams recounted in this book are often referred to as Premonition Dreams, as defined later in the Dream Types section. Although most of the dreams here are of this specific kind, I have also experienced several different types of dreams, such as Past Life Dreams; I have been connected to two of my past lives through my dreams.

No one can interpret my dreams like I can. For me, I know when I am having a premonition dream, because I'm actually playing a role in the dream, like an actor plays a role in a movie. It's like they are branded in my mind, and I can visually see the dreams playing out months and years later through my third eye.

I don't know what it would be like not to dream because I have dreamed premonition dreams all my life. When I have premonition dreams, they will wake me up out of a sound sleep. Once awake, I usually take the time to record my dreams in a journal.

I started keeping a dream journal after so many of my dreams came to fruition. Writing my dreams down in my journal was like therapy for me. By writing them down, it became a way for me to release the images in my head and the anxiety I felt due to what I saw in my dreams. I knew the dreams foretold future events that would take place at a later date. It was also a way for me to validate my dreams.

NOTE FROM THE AUTHOR

*A*ccording to a Newsweek article by Sharon Begley titled, "Why We Believe," ninety percent of Americans believes in the possibility of paranormal or mystical occurrences. While a great majority of these beliefs stem from some sort of religious faith, psychology, and neurology-based scientific research exists a class of spiritually intuitive individuals who utilize the capacity of their minds to channel paranormal experiences (Begley).

As one individual of this growing movement, I would like to present you with my spiritual journey in my book titled, *Believe in Your Dreams*. As the title suggests, my clairvoyant experiences have come in the form of dreams. In the pages that follow recount these dreams and then detail how they came into fruition. Additionally, the book includes trials and tribulations that have served to submerge me more deeply into my spirituality.

Simply put, I am a real person who has experienced the joys as well as the challenges presented by life. While my clairvoyance began at childhood, I did not fully recognize it as a gift until adulthood, and understandably so. From a young age, my experiences with the paranormal were often linked to traumatic incidents such as the kidnapping of my baby sister, my family being in a nearly fatal car accident, the stabbing of my brother, and the murder of my father. In the book I recount each of these instances and the paranormal elements associated with them.

It was not until after my mother lost her battle with breast cancer that I identified my ability as a gift. I realized that not only could I use my premonition dreams to warn and protect friends and family, but I could also reconnect with loved ones through my dreams. Much of the second half of my book recounts such connections with my mother and my father, as well as the loved ones of others.

While the content of this book would most definitely appeal to the paranormal believers, I believe it would be equally appealing to any believer of a higher power. I hope it sparks your interest and allows you to open your mind to the possibilities that lay within yourself.

DREAM TYPES

*T*he different types of dreams and definitions are listed below:

Lucid Dreams - The dreamer becomes aware that he or she is dreaming while the dream is in progress.

Nightmares - A deeply upsetting dream that usually causes strong feelings of fear, sadness, anxiety, and/or horror.

Recurring Dreams - A dream that is experienced repeatedly for a long period of time.

Premonition Dreams - Foretells future events.

Past Life Dreams - A dream that you know is from another lifetime.

When we sleep, we go through five sleep stages. The first stage is light sleep, which is easy for us to wake up from. The second stage is a little deeper sleep. Sleep stages three and four are our deepest state of sleep. When we're sleeping in these stages, our brain activity is gradually slowing down. It's after the fourth sleep stage that we begin rapid eye movement (REM) sleep and is characterized by movements of the eyes. Most dreams take place under REM sleep, but dreams can take place under any of the five stages of sleep. Most dreams last five to twenty minutes.

Our brains cycle through four types of brain waves: delta, theta, alpha, and beta. Each type of brain waves represents a different speed of oscillating electrical voltage in the brain. Delta is the slowest and is present in deep sleep. Theta is present in light sleep. Alpha waves occur during REM sleep. Beta waves, which represent the fastest cycles, are usually only seen in very stressful situations or situations that require very strong mental concentration and focus. The four brain waves make up the electroencephalogram (EEG) (Obringer).

Some dreams are just dreams and nothing more.

Earth

Our Earth is based on solid structures;
therefore it represents stability.

Dreaming of earth can indicate
how secure you feel.

Natural disasters can mean
you are feeling troubled or insecure.

Quiet meadows may mean
you are at peace and relaxed.

CHAPTER ONE

my father kidnapped my baby sister

A couple of months after my parents separated, my mother decided to go back to Atlanta for work, but my brother and I wanted to stay with our grandparents until school was out for the summer. My mother agreed, and she and my baby sister moved back to Atlanta. A few months later, our father called, asking if he could come by and spend time with Missy, my baby sister. Since my mother didn't want to keep our father from seeing my sister, she agreed to the visit and allowed him to take Missy to the store. A couple of hours went by and my mother knew something wasn't right. My father should have brought my sister back home already. She started calling the hospitals in the area, but they had no record of my father or sister being admitted. A while later, my mother started to have a sick feeling in the pit of her stomach and decided to call the police to report that my sister had been kidnapped. My mother kept hoping and praying that he would bring Missy back home, but the days turned into months. My mother was so depressed and concerned about my little sister that she would hardly eat or sleep. She had personally contacted everyone she could think of, including J. Edgar Hoover, to help find Missy. My mother started traveling everywhere looking for my sister; many times she was driving with little or no sleep. Looking for my sister consumed her every waking moment. Our whole family was in such despair over the kidnapping: not because we thought she was in danger or that she wouldn't be taken care of, but because we loved her and missed her so much. There would be times when my mother and grandmother would be gone for days looking for her, spending thousands of dollars along the way.

Six months after the kidnapping, I started having dreams about seeing my father in a store. He was always so excited about seeing me. I would ask him, "Where is Missy?" and he would say, "She is in the trailer down the street." I had other dreams that my father was in the store, and I would again ask him, "Where is Missy?" and he would always give me the same reply, "She's at the trailer." I would wake up very upset and crying. My mother and grandmother asked me what was wrong when I would wake up crying, and I told them about the dreams of my father and sister. The kidnapping was starting to take a toll on me because my brother and I took care of my sister a lot after she was born, especially when our parents had to work on the weekends. Then, I had a dream that I saw my sister and father in a mobile home. Santa Claus was there and my sister was so happy. A few nights later I had another dream. This time, my father and sister were both at the store and my father told me he brought her there every day to get a toy or candy. I kept telling my mother and grandparents about the dreams and how real they were, but, at the time, I really didn't know the importance of the dreams.

Six months after I started having the dreams, my mother, grandparents, uncle, and I decided to take a drive to Chattanooga, Tennessee. It was Mother's Day, and we wanted to ride by my aunt's house to search for my sister. Somehow, I knew my father would be there that day. I expressed these feelings to my mother and grandparents, but I really don't think they put much thought into what I was telling them. As we approached my aunt's house, a little baby girl with blonde hair came running out the front door. My mother immediately turned the car around, and sure enough, it was my sister. I can't explain the excitement we all felt when we realized that this little girl was Missy. My mother rushed down the street to a pay phone and contacted the local authorities. In just a matter of minutes, several police cars showed up and surrounded the house. One policeman knocked on the door and asked if my father was there. After a few minutes, he walked out to where we were, with Missy in his arms, and spoke with my mother and grandparents. I remember being upset and crying. I was excited about us finding my sister, but I was worried about what was going to happen to my father. I could read the sadness and anguish on his face. My father came up and hugged me, saying he loved me very much and that he never meant to hurt anyone. My mother was holding Missy. You could tell she was apprehensive about leaving with us, and she started crying for my father. My father held her for a few minutes to calm her down and then told her that he had to go with the policeman, but he would see her at the police station. My mother had to fill out some paperwork before we could go home.

When we got to the police station, Missy and I were able to spend some time with my father. I started to cry out of worry. My father told me, if I had been there the day he took my baby sister, he would have taken me too. I started talking to him about my dreams and he was amazed. My father told me that my dreams were correct: he lived in a mobile home, and he took Missy to the store every day to buy toys or candy. I went on to tell him that I dreamed he had Santa visit my sister at their trailer during Christmas, and my father said he had done that as well. He told us he had tried to bring Missy back home several times, but she would start crying, saying she wanted to stay with him; he just couldn't bring himself to do it. Before we left the police station, my father hugged me and told me again how much he loved me. He said no matter what, he would always be with me.

On the way home, Missy was really attached to me, not letting me out of her sight, but she was apprehensive with my mother. Her biggest fear had been that my sister would forget who she was because my sister was only one year old at the time of the kidnapping. When we arrived back at my grandparents' home, my brother James was there waiting for us. I will never forget my sister's reaction when she saw him. She just took off running for him. We knew then that she was starting to remember who everyone was and that everything was going to be okay.

After a few months had passed, my mother and sister moved back to Atlanta. James and I stayed with our grandparents until my mother could get settled again. My mother and Missy would come to visit us every week. I finally asked my mother about our father, and she explained to me that he had been sentenced to serve one year in prison for kidnapping my sister, and she filed a restraining order against him. That meant, whenever he was released from prison, he couldn't come anywhere near us. When he was finally released a year later, my mother was scared that he would find out where we lived and try to kidnap my sister again. We missed our father a lot.

When I turned fifteen, I moved back to Atlanta with my mother, but my brother continued to live with our grandparents because he didn't want to leave his friends. Our lives seemed to be pretty normal, and I loved living with my mother and sister. One day I was at a friend's house when the news came on the TV. I saw them rolling a covered body out of a house on a stretcher. All I could see were shoes hanging out of the sheets, but I heard my father's name mentioned. They said he had been shot to death. I jumped up and ran home screaming for my mother, telling her that our father had been shot and killed. My mother called his sister, and she confirmed the news. I will never forget the vision of my father being rolled out on that stretcher. That was one of the worst days of my life.

He had been working as a cook at the Chattanooga Choo Choo in Tennessee and was renting a room from a woman. The day my father was killed, he had just come in after working in the garden all day. There was a knock at the front door, and when my father answered, he saw a man with a gun. He tried to shut the door, but the bullet struck him in his hand, traveled up his arm, through his chest, and out his back, killing him almost instantly. The woman he was renting from heard the commotion and later stated that, when she got to him, my father swallowed one time and he was gone. It was her ex-husband who shot my father.

Little did I know, when my father told me he would always be with us that day at the police station, he really meant it! Shortly after his death, my mother and I started feeling his presence around us. One evening, I was at a friend's house and my mother called to tell me she was sitting in the living room with her drink sitting on the coffee table. All of a sudden, the ice in the drink just started shaking. At the time, we didn't know that was just the beginning of many messages we would receive from my father from the other side. I started having visitation dreams from my father. In these dreams my father was always standing outside my bedroom window and would reassure me that he was there, watching over us and protecting us.

CHAPTER TWO

my uncle and his family in a serious car accident

$\mathcal{I}$ n 1972, at the age of fifteen, I dreamed that my uncle and his family were in a car accident and they all had serious injuries. In the dream, my cousin Chris died in the accident. I ended up at the cemetery at my cousin's grave reading his headstone. Then, Chris appeared in my dream. I started talking to him and realized he was alive. The next morning, when I woke up, I knew the dream had a meaning, but I tried to push it out of my mind. When I had dreams like this, I thought if I didn't say them out loud, it would keep the dreams from coming true. I was living with my grandparents at the time. That morning, my family was going to the flea market. Before we left the house, I told my grandparents to be sure to the leave the door key because my mother would be coming today. My grandparents asked if I had spoken with my mother as she had not told anyone else that she was planning a visit. I told them I had not, but I just knew she was coming. I kept telling everyone throughout the day that my mother was coming. When we returned from the flea markets, I started studying for a test for school, and my granddaddy quizzed me. The phone rang and my grandmother answered it. We could tell she was upset, so we ran into the living room to see what was going on. My grandmother hung up the phone and said, "That was the hospital calling to say that Junior and his whole family have been in a bad car accident."

My grandfather called his cousin Mildred and gave her the news about my uncle. As we rushed out the door, I told my grandparents again to leave the door key for my mother. On the way to the hospital, the only thing I could think of was the dream I'd had the night before and how scared I was. I didn't know what to expect when we entered the hospital, but I knew it wasn't going to be good. When we arrived, my grandfather asked where my uncle and his family were. They took us to my aunt Katie, who was lying on a stretcher in the hallway. She had her front teeth knocked out, a broken jaw, a fractured ankle, and broken ribs. She was in a lot of pain and started crying, saying that she didn't know the condition of my uncle or the kids. She asked my granddaddy to find out what he could. The only thing my aunt knew was that they had to cut my uncle out of the car. When my granddaddy came back, the look on his face said it all.

Granddaddy told us that the steering wheel had gone through my uncle's chest and that he was in critical condition. My cousin Chris was still being treated, and he was also considered to be in serious condition with fractures to both legs and his pelvis. Chris's brother Ronnie was getting a CT scan to check for a concussion, but, so far, Ronnie's injuries were the least severe. A few minutes later, a policeman came up and told us that they had been driving on a very dark, curvy road when my uncle lost control of the car and hit a tree.

After being at the hospital for a couple of hours, my mother showed up and I could read the fear on her face while we updated her on the condition of her brother and his family. While we were waiting on more information from the doctors, I told my mother that I had known she was coming home. My granddaddy asked my mother how she knew we were at the hospital. She told us that, shortly after she arrived to an empty house, Mildred called over to check if anyone was there because I'd been so persistent about her coming home. Mildred had the shock of her life when my mother actually picked up the phone. After several hours had passed, the doctors finally came and updated us on the condition of all our family members. They advised us to go home and get some rest because we would have some long days ahead of us.

When we got home that night, my mother started telling us why she decided to come home. She had gone to a dance club and saw a man on the dance floor that reminded her of her brother. All of a sudden, she had an urge to get home. She couldn't explain the urgency to her manager when she called to inform him of her trip, but she just knew she had to get home. My mother went on to tell us that when she came into town, she had to pass the road which led to my uncle's house and had thought about stopping by his house first, but instead she decided to go straight to my grandparent's house. Once my mother arrived and found that nobody was at home, she knew something wasn't right. A few minutes later, my granddaddy's cousin called and gave her the news about her brother and his family.

A week or so later, my uncle was taken out of intensive care and put into a private room. My cousin Chris had surgery on his pelvis and was going to need to be put in a body cast from his waist down for the next several months. My aunt was still in the hospital recovering from her injuries. We ended up having relatives on three different floors of the hospital. We practically lived at the hospital for the next couple of weeks, spending as much time as possible with our family members.

While my mother and I were visiting my aunt Katie, giving her an update on the condition of my uncle, she told us that my uncle had been wearing his favorite shirt on the day of the accident. She wanted to get him another shirt just like it. My mother made it her mission to find that shirt. She finally found the exact shirt. I think my mom finding that shirt did more good for my aunt than any of the pain medicine she had been given by the doctors.

Our family members appeared to be on the mend, until one day, as my mother and I were visiting my uncle, he started saying he was burning up, which was strange because we were both freezing. A few minutes later, he asked us who the lady was, dressed in black, standing at the foot of his bed. We thought the pain medicine my uncle was taking was making him hallucinate. What freaked me out even more was that I was going to be spending the next couple of nights at the hospital with him in order to keep a watch on him and everyone else. That night, he started complaining again that he was hot, but I was still freezing. He kept asking, "Who is the lady, dressed in black, standing at the foot of my bed?" I kept explaining that I didn't see anyone, and we thought the medicine was making him hallucinate. He insisted that the lady was always standing at the foot of his bed.

The next morning, when my grandparents and my mother came to hospital, I told them about my night with my uncle. My grandparents discussed their concerns with the nurse and the doctors, who agreed that, while my uncle's condition was improving, the medicine was causing my uncle to feel hot and hallucinate. Throughout the day, my uncle's condition appeared to be improving, so instead of staying another night at the hospital, I decided to go home to get some rest. The hospital assured my grandparents that if anything happened during the night, they would call.

My mother, sister, and I were sleeping when, at two in the morning, the phone rang. My mother jumped out of bed, racing to get to the phone because she thought it was the hospital calling us about one of our family members. I heard my mother talking on the phone, asking questions about my uncle and the rest of our family members.

A couple of seconds later, I heard my granddaddy say, "Betty who are you talking to?" My mother replied, "I'm talking to Rhonda." My granddaddy came and opened the bedroom door to confirm that I was, in fact, in the bed. I finally got up and went into the living room. My granddaddy asked my mother about the phone call. She told us that she asked how Uncle was doing, and the person replied he, Aunt Katie, and Chris were all resting well. After checking on everyone, the person decided to go downstairs to get a soda. My mother insisted that it was me on the phone the whole time. The only family members not staying at my grandparents' house were currently admitted in the hospital, so we had no other family members that could have made the mysterious phone call.

The next morning my grandparents went to the hospital ahead of us. A few hours later, my grandmother called saying that my uncle had taken a turn for the worse. He had started suffocating and was rushed to x-ray, where they discovered that his lungs were full of blood. He had almost died. Once my uncle's lungs were cleared, he never talked about seeing the lady in black again, but to this day, he still remembers her standing guard at the foot of his bed.

1972

I had a dream that my uncle and
his whole family was in a car accident.
In my dreams It was a horrible accident
and my cousin Chris was killed. I remember
standing at his grave and was in so much
Grief and felt so sad, then all of a sudden
I realized Chris was okay and I
was so happy.

PART 2 - Actual Events
   The next morning when I woke up
my grandparents, uncle, mildred and smiley
were suppose to Go to some flea markets.
I kept Telling my grandparents to be
sure they leave the key outside for
mom, because she will be coming home
today from Sailsbury, NC. Everyone
looked at me as if I was crazy, but
I was persistant that mom would be
there today so my grandparents left
the key on the front porch column.
When we came home from the flea
market my mom still hadn't arrived
but I knew she would. I started
studying for a test that I was having
at school the next day and my
grandfather was quizzing me. The
phone rang at my grandparents
home and IT was the hospital calling telling
us that my uncle and his family was

IN A CAR accident and his whole family was in the process of being checked out and admitted and for us to GET TO THE hospital ASAP!)

My grandfather then made a call to Mildred (his cuisin) and told her about the accident and that we were heading up to the hospital. Before we left, I again told my grandparents to leave the key for mom. On the way to the hospital all I could Think about was the dream I had the night before. SiNCE I was a little girl I would dream things that would happen. I Remember telling my mom I was scared to go to BED BECAUSE of my DREAMS.

When we made IT to THE HospiTAL They had my uncle's whole family laid out on beds IN THE HALLway EXCEPT for my uncle & my cuisin CHris They were the most serious of THE 7 of them. MY AuNT HAD HER TEETH BusTED out AND IEG AND ANKLE INJURIES. WE REAlly DiDN'T KNOW THE EXTENT of MY uNCLE & CHris INJURIES WE JuST KNEW they were serius.

CHAPTER THREE

the phone call from my father from the other side

Two o'clock on a Saturday morning, my phone rang. I picked the phone up on the first ring, and as soon as I heard the voice on the other end of the phone, I realized it was my father, who had been killed years before. He was calling to warn me of an event that was going to take place at a later date. At the time, I didn't know exactly what was going to happen, but I knew it wasn't good news. While my father was talking to me on the phone, I had an intense feeling of sadness and just wanted to cry. I was on the phone for about three minutes or so. When the conversation ended, I hung up and drifted back to sleep.

The next morning, I was talking to my mother and told her I had dreamed that my father called me. My mother looked at me and said, "Rhonda, that wasn't a dream." My mother went on to say that the phone rang one time in the middle of the night, and I'd answered it on the very first ring. She heard me say hello, but she never heard me say another word. I told her how I felt while I was on the phone and that whatever he told me made me want to cry. Once my mother confirmed that the phone call was real and not just a dream, we both knew that my father was still guiding and protecting us from the other side. I tried to put the phone call out of my mind, even though I knew that something was going to happen. Something that would explain what my father was trying so desperately to warn me about.

A week later, I went on a trip with my boyfriend and his parents to visit their relatives in Louisiana. I was very excited about the trip, even though I had never been away from home without my family before. When we arrived in Louisiana, I started feeling homesick, became very emotional, and just started crying. I tried to hide my feelings from everyone except my boyfriend because I didn't want to spoil the trip for everyone else. We had been in Louisiana for a couple of days when I received a phone call from my mother saying that my brother had been in a serious motorcycle accident. His leg was broken in several places, among other injuries, and they had to put a screw in his leg; it would be in traction for quite some time. I asked her how the accident happened. She said that my brother was running from the police when he crashed the motorcycle and went up under a mobile home. The doctors and the policeman told my mother that James was lucky he survived the accident. Then, my mother told me that the accident happened Saturday morning at two o'clock, the exact same day and time of the phone call I received from my father. Finally, I realized this is what my father was trying to warn me about, from the other side.

PHONE CALL FROM DAD FROM THE OTHER SIDE.

ONE NIGHT AT 2:40 AM I THOUGHT I HAD A DREAM THAT THE PHONE BESIDE MY BED RUNG AND I REMEMBER IT RINGING ONE TIME AND SO I PICKED THE PHONE UP AND I KNEW IT WAS MY FATHER'S VOICE ON THE OTHER END TELLING ME SOMETHING WAS GOING TO HAPPEN BUT I DIDN'T REALLY KNOW WHAT. I FELT LIKE CRYING WHEN I HUNG THE PHONE UP.
THE NEXT MORNING I TOLD MY MOM & I HAD THE STRANGEST DREAM AND SHE SAID, HONEY THE PHONE DID RING LAST NIGHT AND YOU PICKED IT UP ON THE FIRST RING AND SHE HEARD ME SAY HELLO BUT SHE NEVER HEARD ME SAY ANOTHER WORD AFTER THAT.

CHAPTER FOUR

*my brother was stabbed eight times
by three strangers*

*J*n December 1976, I had a dream that three men were attacking my brother. Throughout the entire dream, I was trying to get to my brother because I knew the men were trying to kill him. This dream seemed like it went on for hours. When I finally woke up, I was scared and couldn't get my brother off my mind. I thought that if I didn't say anything about the dream the dream wouldn't come true, so I never discussed the dream with anyone, not even my husband. My husband and I had only been married a few months, and I never really talked much to him about my dreams because I didn't want him to think I was crazy. My mother was the only person I felt comfortable discussing my dreams with because I knew she wouldn't judge me. My mother understood. She knew I had a special gift and tried to console me the best she could. A couple of weeks after the dream about my brother, the phone rang in the middle of the night. It was my grandmother on the other end of the phone, and I could tell by the sound of her voice that something was wrong. My grandmother told me that my brother had been stabbed and was in the hospital, but the doctors didn't know the extent of his injuries. I told my grandmother I would be there within an hour. When I finally reached the hospital, my mother was standing by my brother's bed staring at all the bandages covering his back. She told me the nurse had just given my brother something for pain. I can remember her reaching for the cross hanging from her necklace. If it hadn't been for the policeman who saw the attack while passing by in his patrol car, the three men would have killed my brother. When the policeman arrived on the scene, he thought James had just been beaten until he noticed that James's shirt was covered in blood. He then saw multiple stab wounds to his back. James had to be strapped down to keep him from further injuring himself.

While waiting for my brother to recover in the hospital, my mother told me how she learned about the attack. She said,

> "The knock on my front door echoed throughout the apartment, waking me from a sound sleep. The clock on my dresser read 2:30 a.m. Instinct told me that something had to be wrong. I slipped on my

slippers and padded toward the door. When I threw the door open, the sight of my brother and his wife standing on the porch caused my knees to shake. Something had to be terribly wrong for them to wake me during the night.

Silently they entered the living room and sat on the sofa. Everything was deathly quiet as my brother kept staring at the Christmas tree I had put up several days earlier. It seemed forever before he finally spoke. 'James has been hurt,' he said in a low voice, still not meeting my eyes. 'He was beaten and stabbed by three drunken men. I don't know how badly he is injured. He was still in the emergency room when I left the hospital.'

My eyes fell on a brightly wrapped gift under the tree. It belonged to my twenty-one-year-old son James. It had taken hours of time to find the perfect gift. Now it might never be opened. Oh, God, how could you let this happen? I thought.

Finally, I found the strength to stumble to the bedroom and change clothes, all the time dreading what I would find when I reached the hospital. Still unable to speak, I walked to the front door with my brother. Suddenly, I remembered the silver necklace with a small cross that I had placed on the coffee table earlier. Even though I was still numb with shock, I crossed the room, picked up the necklace, and hooked it around my neck. Although I was in a hurry to reach the hospital, I was still so afraid. What if James was dead when I got there? How could I bear losing my only son?

After what seemed an eternity, we reached the hospital. My hands shook as I opened the emergency door. Oh, God, please let him still be alive, I prayed. The nurse was very kind when I asked her about James, but her kindness did not soften the pain in my heart when she told me my son had been badly beaten and stabbed eight times in the back. 'He has been taken up to his room,' she said in a gentle voice. 'His vital signs are stable, but he could have internal injuries that we don't know about.'

Nothing could have prepared me for what I found when I entered my son's room. His once strong body was curled in agony. My heart broke as I looked at the bandages covering his back. He twisted and turned on the bed, in too much pain to know I was there. With shaking fingers, I reached up and grasped the silver cross, trying to gather enough strength to face the long night ahead.

Just when I thought I could bear no more, the cross seemed to come alive in my hand, sending rays of heat throughout my body. Suddenly, I knew that I was not alone; God was with me. Regardless of what lay ahead, he would be there, lending me his strength and support.

It was the longest night of my life, not knowing if James would live until morning. But, just when I thought the night would never end, a streak of light came floating across the horizon. Even though dawn had brought a new day, it had also brought an even greater fear when I realized that James had stopped moaning.

Fear flooded my entire body. Somehow, I managed to get to my feet and walk the few steps to his bed. James looked so pitifully small lying in that large hospital bed. A thousand memories ran through my mind like the times I had to spank him during his childhood, and the many times he and his sister had fought over which cartoon to watch on television. It was these memories that kept me from noticing immediately the rise and fall of his chest. There is no explaining how I felt when I realized my son was still alive. 'Thank you, God,' I whispered.

The next morning, it was no surprise when the doctor told me James had no internal injuries and would be fine. After all, a greater power had already made his presence known. God's presence was felt by the whole family a few weeks later as we gathered around the Christmas tree with James. We had finally come to realize what Christmas was really all about. God had shown us the real spirit of Christmas. It was a special time for loving and giving, and God had given me the life of my only son."

1976

I dreamed that 3 men was attacking my brother and in my Dream I was trying to get to him, because I knew they were trying to kill him. I was frantic and then I woke up, the dream seemed to go for hours.

CHAPTER FIVE

an earthquake in the U.S.

ebruary 28, 2010: I was in Chicago visiting with family and dreamed I was on the third floor of an office building when an earthquake hit. After the earthquake was over, I was looking around at the damage. I could feel the terror and the fear of the people around me. All the windows were shattered and much of the walls were missing. I looked down at the floor seeing a huge crack, and could tell the building wasn't stable. I knew the authorities were trying to figure out how to get us down from the building. I felt as if my family members were all around me. I don't know if they were standing on the ground below trying to communicate with me, or if some of them were actually in the building with me. I remember going to the edge of the building where the windows were shattered and looking down, shouting to the people on the ground. As I was bent over, I lost my footing and started to fall. I reached and grabbed some type of debris, which resembled a long rope, hanging from the side of the building. After that, I woke up. The next morning, I told my husband, son, and his girlfriend about my dream and that I hoped the dream wouldn't come true. It was hard for me to get the dream off my mind that day, no matter how hard I tried.

On March 4th, I was listening to my friend Mary Occhino's live radio show. She is an intuitive/medium who has a live show on Sirius radio called, "Angels on Call." Her son, Chris Corry, was on the show to discuss the paranormal. They started talking about all the earthquakes around the world, and, at that moment, I knew I needed to call Mary's show to tell her and Chris about my earthquake dream. I called in and started relaying the details of my dream. Mary started asking me questions: if it was warm or hot at the time of the quake - I told her I thought the weather was warm because I think I had short sleeves on; where I thought the quake occurred-I wasn't sure but it seemed like Los Angeles. She told me she was seeing me at the place of the earthquake. She wrote the location down on paper and showed it to her son, but she didn't want to say the location out loud. She went on to say that, while not many people can predict earthquakes, she felt that I had a gift. Weeks went by. I was still bothered about the earthquake dream and couldn't get it off my mind.

On Sunday, April 4, 2010, a magnitude 7.2 earthquake struck Baja, California. The city sustained structural damage, broken windows, leaking gas lines, and damage to the water system. The powerful earthquake in Baja, California rocked the U.S./Mexico border region, collapsing a parking structure south of the border, and causing power outages in both countries. It sent out seismic waves felt from Las Vegas, to Los Angeles, to Arizona. It was the largest earthquake in the region in nearly eighteen years.

I called my friend Mary Occhino and asked her if this was the earthquake in my dream. She said yes, it was.

Wind

Air is all around us, it is our ideas and
feelings and our expressions.
Our words are carried by air.

The clarity of the air in your dreams can
represent how clear you are thinking
cloudy or smoky skies may represent that
you are distracted.

Air is also forceful-wind.
This can symbolize energy.
Think about a summer day on the beach
with a nice breeze versus a hurricane.

We also use air to breathe and if you dream
of choking or suffocating you may
subconsciously be feeling you are not being
heard or have enough expression.

CHAPTER SIX

my childhood home was haunted by spirits

*W*hen I was little, my parents, brother, and I moved to a new house. The first time I walked into the house, I didn't want to be there; I could feel something wasn't right. I never wanted to sleep in my bedroom by myself, but my parents thought I was a typical three-year-old who was scared all the time. One night, I was asleep and something woke me up. I saw a hand coming through my bedroom window. I was so scared; I started screaming for my parents. They came running into my room and I told them what I had seen. They told me that it was just a bad dream, but to this day, I can still feel how terrified I was of that room. My mother slept in the bed with me the rest of that night.

The next day, we went to visit my grandparents. My mother told them about my dream and how terrified I was. When it came time for us to leave later that evening, I started crying hysterically and told my parents I didn't want to go back, but, of course, I had to go back to that dreaded house. My parents just kept telling me that I had a bad dream and nothing was going to hurt me. A couple of days later, I was sleeping and found myself all tangled up in the covers. It felt as if someone, or something, was holding the covers down so I couldn't get out. I was terrified because I wasn't able to breathe, so I started screaming. My father ran in my bedroom and tried to get the covers off of me as fast as he could, but even he had a hard time removing the covers. The whole time I just kept screaming. After that night, I never slept in that bedroom again. I really believe that night had an impact on my parents, prompting our move shortly thereafter. There are not enough words to describe the relief I felt about leaving that house.

On April 17, 2009, I was going to meet my family for a visit. I planned to swing by my brother's house, on the way, to pick him up. When I got there, I couldn't find my brother's house, so I called him and he said, "Rhonda you have to go by the house where you saw the hand coming through the window." I explained to James that I didn't remember where the house was, so he gave me directions. After picking him up, we drove down the street and he pointed to the house where we used to live. I told him that the house was evil.

Wednesday, April 29, 2009, I dreamed that I was at a familiar place and the Ku Klux Klan was there. They started to leave, but turned to me and said they would be back in three hours. Then, all of a sudden, several hundred African-Americans- women, men, and children of all ages- started coming to the same familiar place, and I knew they were in danger. I was so scared for them. All I wanted was to get them out of harm's way. The African-American people would not leave, no matter how much I warned them about the danger that awaited them if they stayed. A few minutes later, I could see the headlights of motorcycles coming up the roadway and I saw the white robes of the KKK. I kept telling everyone they needed to leave, but they never left. Shortly after the arrival of the KKK, the fighting started.

I really didn't know the true meaning of the dream until the next day when I called my dear friend Mary Occhino during her live radio show. I never mentioned my dream about the KKK to her that I had the night before. I actually called her to tell her about the experiences I'd had in regards to the evil house from my childhood. I wanted to see if she could shed more light on what I experienced as a young girl. I went on to tell Mary that I was terrified of this house, about the hand I saw coming through my bedroom window, and how I had been wrapped up in the sheets and couldn't get out. Mary told me I was having a psychic/medium experience and that I was picking up on the negative energy of the property. She further explained that she was seeing killings, brutality, burnings of crosses, and hangings by the hands of the KKK. Immediately, I told Mary about the dream I'd had the night before.

Mary went on to say that a lot of the souls were still trapped on the property because when people die in such a violent way, it's not easy for them to cross over to the other side. She said the hand I saw as a child was the hand of evil. She said there were hundreds of murders that took place on the property. She asked me and other listeners to pray for the souls trapped on the property, or to meditate on them to help them cross over to the other side. Another listener called in after my call and commented about my experience. Mary said not only did she see the burning crosses as we discussed my story, but she also smelled the burning flesh.

Later, while I was speaking with a coworker about my dream and my conversation with Mary, she told me there had been an execution of a white supremacist at the Georgia Diagnostic and Classification Prison in Jackson, Georgia the night before. She said the member of the KKK that was executed could have had ties to Rome some way because she thought he was from Athens, GA.

*

4/30/09

ACTUAL EVENT

I CALLED MARY O TO ASK HER
ABOUT THIS HOUSE I LIVED IN
WHEN I WAS 2-3 YRS OLD. I WAS
TERRIFIED OF THIS HOUSE. ONE NIGHT
I SAW A HAND COME THROUGH THE
WINDOW WHICH TERRIFIED ME TO NO
END. ANOTHER NIGHT I WOKE UP
AND I WAS WRAPPED UP IN THE
SHEETS AND IT FELT AS IF SOMEONE
WAS HOLDING THE SHEETS SO I
COULDN'T GET OUT. I REALLY THOUGHT
I WAS GOING TO DIE BECAUSE I
COULDN'T BREATH, I REMEMBER
SCREAMING AND CRYING AND MY
FATHER RUSHED IN TO MY ROOM
AND HE EVEN HAD TROUBLE GETTING
ME OUT OF THE SHEETS. I WAS
TERRIFIED OF THIS HOUSE. MARY O
TOLD ME I WAS HAVING A PSYCHIC/MEDIUM
EXPERIENCE AND I WAS PICKING UP
ON THE NEGATIVE ENERGY ON THE
PROPERTY. MARY O WENT ON TO
SAY THAT SHE WAS PICKING UP

Activity, Killings, Brutality, Burnings of crosses and hangings by the hands of KKK. Immediately I told Mary about my dream the night before about the KKK and I was telling the black people they needed to leave because the KKK would be back in a hour or so, but they didn't leave in time and they were involved in some major fighting. Mary O went on to say that a lot of the souls are still on that property because when people dies in such a violet way it's not easy for them to go over to the other side. Mary said there were hundreds of murders in this location. Mary asked everyone to pray for the souls left on this property or to meditate on them. Another caller called in and was talking about my story and Mary O said she didn't just see the burning crosses but she actually smelled the burning flesh.

WHEN I TOLD MARY ABOUT MY
DREAM THE NIGHT BEFORE, SHE
SAID I WAS MEANT TO FIND OUT
THE INFORMATION TODAY.
I TOLD MARY O THAT I HAD
STARTED THINKING ABOUT THIS HOUSE
A MONTH AGO BUT I DION'T
KNOW WHERE THE HOUSE WAS AT
BECAUSE I WAS TO YOUNG TO
REMEMBER. BUT I HAD WENT TO
ROME ON APRIL 17TH 2009 I WAS
GOING TO PICK MY BROTHER UP AND
COULD FIND HIS LOCATION SO AFTER
CALLING MY BROTHER FOR DIRECTIONS
HE SAID, RHONDA YOU PASS THE HOUSE
THAT YOU SAW THE HAND COMING OUT
THE WINDOW AND I WENT ON TO
TELL HIM I DION'T REMEMBER
WHERE THE HOUSE WAS. HE GAVE ME
DIRECTIONS SO I PICKED HIM UP AND
AS WE PASSED THE HOUSE HE SHOWED
ME THE HOUSE AND I TOLD HIM
THERE WAS SOMETHING EVIL THERE

AND HE SAID YOU WERE JUST
SCARED AND I TOLD HIM AGAIN
THERE WAS SOMETHING EVIL THERE
AND I TOLD HIM I SHOULD TAKE
A PICTURE OF THE HOUSE AND HE
ASKED ME WHY AND I SAID
AGAIN THERE IS SOMETHING EVIL
THERE. I THOUGHT I WOULD TAKE
A PICTURE WHEN I WOULD BRING
HIM HOME BUT I NEVER WENT BY
THE HOUSE AGAIN BECAUSE HE
STAYED W/ HIS EX FATHER-IN-LAW
THAT NIGHT.
      LATER ON APRIL 30TH I TOLD
ONE OF MY CO-WORKERS ABOUT
MY CALL W/ MARY O AND SHE TOLD
ME A EX MEMBER OF THE KKK
WAS EXECUTED ON APRIL 29TH AROUND
7:00 PM. MY FRIEND DONNA DIDN'T
THINK THAT WA COCIDENCE EITHER.
SHE SAID THE MAN THAT WAS EXECUTED
MIGHT HAVE HAD TIES TO RME SOME
WAY BECAUSE SHE THOUGHT HE WAS
FROM ATHENS, GA.

SIGNS

THROUGH ALL OF THIS INFORMATION
GOD AND MY ANGELS HAD
SHOWED ME SIGNS I HAD ASKED FOR
I TOLD GOD AND THE ANGELS I WAS
READY TO OPEN AND READY TO RECEIVE
MESSAGES FROM SPIRIT'S THAT NEEDED
MY HELP AND I WAS READY TO HELP
PEOPLE ON THIS EARTH TO RECEIVE
MESSAGES FROM THE OTHER SIDE.
GOD AND THE ANGELS BROUGHT ME
100'S OF SPIRITS ON APRIL 29TH
FOR ME TO HELP TO FIND PEACE.

WHEN I WAS TALKING TO MARY
ABOUT MY EXPERIENCES AND
MY DREAM THE NIGHT BEFORE
I TOLD MARY, I WAS SO
OVERWHELMED AT THE MOMENT
BECAUSE I WAS PICKING UP THE
FEELINGS FROM ALL THE SOULS
ON THAT PROPERTY.

CHAPTER SEVEN

michael jackson's death

On June, 20, 2009, I dreamed that my son, Jordan Michael, myself, and Michael Jackson were walking together on the sidewalk at Michael Jackson's Neverland Ranch. We were just walking and talking, enjoying each other's company. I remember later in the dream, I was concerned that my son was with Michael because of all the molestation allegations that had been brought against Michael in the past years. Then I realized, my son is a third-degree black belt and he can take care of himself. When I woke up, I couldn't understand why I dreamed that Jordan and I were with Michael at his Neverland

Ranch. I'm sad to say that I dismissed the entire dream.

Over the next few days, I started feeling like someone had run over me with a Mack truck. I was feeling lifeless. I would go home and go straight to bed. My friend and I were supposed to go walking on the Wednesday before Michael's death, but I called her and cancelled because I was feeling so strange. I told my coworkers something wasn't right and I was feeling really out of sorts. I know that whenever I experience those feelings, it is a warning to prepare me for what lies ahead.

On June 25th, my husband, mother-in-law, and I were out to dinner when the news of Michael Jackson's passing came across the TV. We were all in shock over his death. That evening at home, I couldn't stop thinking of my dream about Michael a few days prior to his passing. Things started to make sense to me; at that point, I knew I was picking up Michael's energy. My friend Mary Occhino was doing a tribute to Michael on her June 26th radio show, so I called Mary and told her about my dream. Mary said I was picking up on Michael's feelings regarding the molestation charges. She went on to tell me that it was a premonition dream; it was Michael's destiny. Mary then told me that she had been feeling out of sorts, as if she had been depressed. I told Mary I had been feeling the same way. After Michael's death, he came to me a couple of times in my dreams, as if he was trying to tell me something. To this day, I feel that Michael wanted to be buried at his Neverland Ranch. Michael continues to visit me in my dreams.

FRIDAY JUNE 20, 2009

I DREAMED THAT MY SON JORDAN MICHAEL, MICHAEL JACKSON AND MYSELF WAS AT MICHAELS NEVERLAND RANCH. WE WERE WALKING THROUGHOUT NEVERLAND TALKING AND ENJOYING EACH OTHERS COMPANY.

LATER IN MY DREAM I WAS CONCERNED THAT MY SON WAS GOING TO HANG OUT WITH MICHAEL JACKSON BECAUSE OF ALL THE MOLESTATION ALLEGATIONS THAT HAD BEEN BROUGHT AGAINST MICHAEL IN THE PAST YEARS. THEN I REALIZED MY SON IS A THIRD DEGREE BLACK BELT AND HE CAN TAKE CARE OF HIMSELF. WHEN I WOKE UP I COULDN'T UNDERSTAND WHY I DREAMED THAT JORDAN AND I WERE WITH MICHAEL AT HIS NEVERLAND RANCH AND I'M SAD TO SAY THAT I DISMISSED THE ENTIRE DREAM. I DIDN'T KNOW THE IMPORTANCE OF THIS DREAM UNTIL 6/25/09 WHEN MY HUSBAND, MOTHER IN LAW AND I WERE AT DINNER WHEN THE NEWS OF MICHAEL JACKSON'S PASSING CAME ACROSS THE TV.

ACTUAL EVENT 2009
FRIDAY JUNE 26TH I CALLED
MARY D AND TOLD HER ABOUT MY
DREAM AND THAT I FELT I HAD
MISS UNDERSTOD MY DREAM ABOUT
MICHAEL JACKSON IN RELATION TO
MY SON JORDAN MICHAEL. AND THAT
THE WHOLE TIME I WAS DREAMING OF
JORDAN BEING W/ MICHAEL IT HAD
NOTHING TO DO W/ THE MOLESTATION
BUT IT WAS A WARNING THAT
MICHAEL JACKSON WAS GOING TO
DIE AND THAT IS WHY THE DREAM
WAS BOTHERING ME SO MUCH. MARY
SAID SHE THOUGHT THAT I HAD FORESEEN
WHAT WAS MICHAEL DEATH. MARY
WAS SAYING THIS WHOLE WEEK SHE
HAD BEEN FEELING OUT OF SORTS AS
IF SHE HAD BEEN DEPRESSED OR SOMETHING.
I TOLD MARY THIS WHOLE WEEK
I WAS HAVING TO GO HOME AND GO
STRAIGHT TO BED BECAUSE I HAD
BEEN FEELING SO BAD. MARY SAID
SHE HAD BEEN DOING THE SAME THING

DURING I STARTED FEELING
SOME BETTER ON WEDNESDAY
BUT WAS VERY DRAINED.
THURSDAY I WAS STILL FEELING
TIRED. BUT I SEEMED TO BE
IMPROVING. I REMEMBER TELLING
MY FRIENDS AT WORK ON TUESDAY
I FELT LIKE I HAD BEEN RAN
OVER BY A TRUCK AND WAS
FEELING LIFELESS. I WAS SUPPOSE
TO WALK W/ MY FRIEND TEE
BUT CALLED OFF THE WALK
BECAUSE I WAS FEELING SO
STRANGE.
MARY'S SHOW WAS DEVOTED
TO MICHAEL JACKSON TODAY
I RECORDED THE ENTIRE SHOW
ON MY MP3 PLAYER.

11/28/11 MONDAY 2:00 AM
I DREAMED THAT MICHAEL JACKSON
WAS PUTTING ON A SHOW AND MY
SON JORDAN AND I WERE STANDING
IN SOME TYPE OF ROADWAY WAITING
FOR THE SHOW TO START. A FEW
MINUTES LATER MICHAEL JACKSON
CAME OUT TO START THE SHOW AND
I YELLED TO HIM AND MICHAEL ACKNOWLEDGED
ME. MICHAEL WENT STARTED TO SING AND
SOMETHING WASN'T TO HIS LIKING AND
HE STOPPED SINGING AND WAS TRYING
TO CORRECT THE PROBLEM AND HE WAS
TALKING ABOUT THE SONG AND WAS
TELLING PEOPLE IN HIS SHOW SOMETHING
ABOUT THE SONG THAT THE SIZZLE HAS
TO BE CORRECT JUST LIKE IN HIS MOVIE
THIS IS IT! MICHAEL KEPT TRYING
TO START THE SHOW BUT KEPT STOPPING
IN THE MIDDLE BECAUSE SOMETHING
WASN'T RIGHT. IT WAS AS IF
MICHAEL COULDN'T GET IT RIGHT OR HAD
SELF DOUBT. ————————>

11/28/11   2:10 Am.

WHEN I SAW THAT MICHAEL KEPT HAVING PROBLEMS I YELLED OUT TO MICHAEL AGAIN TELLING HIM HE COULD DO IT AND TO TRY AND GIVE HIM ENCOURAGEMENT. MICHAEL WALKED OVER TO ME AND RIGHT AWAY I NOTICED HOW YOUNG HE LOOKED. HIS SKIN WAS CLEAR AND SMOOTH, HIS NOSE WAS NORMAL LIKE IT WAS WHEN HE WAS YOUNGER IN HIS TEENS OR 20'S. HIS HAIR WAS MORE CURLY. I REMEMBER TELLING MICHAEL TO GO OUT THERE AND JUST SANG AND TO SHOW EVERYONE HOW GOOD HE IS. THE NEXT THING I KNOW I'M IN THIS RESTAURANT AND THIS OTHER LADY WAS TALKING ABOUT MICHAEL JACKSON SAYING SHE HAD A DREAM ABOUT MICHAEL TOO.

A FEW MINUTES LATER I WAS SITTING ON A PORCH ON SOME TYPE OF SOFA W/ MY DAUGHTER

11/28/11 MONDAY

AND MICHAEL CAME AND SAT DOWN
BESIDE MY DAUGHTER. AND I LEANED
OVER MY DAUGHTER TO TALK TO MICHAEL
AND I TOLD HIM YOU LOOK EXACTLY
LIKE I SAW HIM IN MY DREAM
AND MICHAEL RESPONDED REALLY.
AND I WAS COMPLIMENTING MICHAEL
ON HIS LOOKS. I PROCEEDED TO TELL MICHAEL
THIS DREAM WOKE ME UP AND
I FELT LIKE MICHAEL WAS IN THE
ROOM W/ME. IT TOOK ME AWHILE
TO FALL MADE TO SLEEP THINKING
ABOUT MICHAEL BECAUSE I FELT
LIKE THERE WAS A MESSAGE FOR ME
ME IN THE DREAM. AS I'M SITTING
HERE AT WORK WRITING IN MY DREAM
JOURNAL THEY ANNOUNCED THAT CONRAD
MURRAY WILL BE SENTENCED TODAY
11/29/11 IN THE DEATH OF MICHAEL JACKSON.
I FOUND IT ODD THAT MY SON JORDAN
WAS IN THIS DREAM JUST LIKE THE
OTHER DREAM I HAD OF MICHAEL. MY SON'S →

11/28/11. MEMORY 2:00 AM
JORDAN'S MIDDLE NAME IS MICHAEL.
I FEEL LIKE THERE IS SOME TYPE
OF SOUL CONNECTION BETWEEN MICHAEL,
MYSELF AND MY SON JORDAN.
THE OTHER CONNECTION IS MY
MOTHER'S MAIDEN NAME IS
JACKSON.
 I KEPT THINKING TO MYSELF
WHY DAKOTA WASN'T IN THE DREAM
BECAUSE SHE LOVES MICHAEL JACKSON.
I DON'T THINK MY GRANDDAUGHTER
BEING MICHAEL JACKSON FOR HALLOWEEN
WAS A FLUKE I THINK THERE IS
ALSO A SOUL CONNECTION THERE AS
WELL. MY GRANDDAUGHTER BIRTHDAY
IS SEPT. 23RD AND SHE ALSO HAD
A MICHAEL JACKSON BIRTHDAY CAKE.
IN THE MEAN TIME MICHAEL JACKSON'S
DEATH TRIAL IS TAKING PLACE AT
THE SAME TIME. THERE IS A
HIGHER SOURCE AT WORK HERE.
CONRAD MURRAY WAS FOUND GUILTY OF INVOLUNTARY
MANSLAUGHTER

CHAPTER EIGHT

a visit from popsi

*N*ovember 3, 2009: My father-in-law, Carlos, "Popsi" (as we called him) paid me a visit in my dreams. Popsi is the greatest father-in-law anyone could ever dream of having. He is such a kind and loving person. Popsi and my mother-in-law welcomed me into their family with open arms thirty-six years ago and both are like parents to me. I dreamed that my mother-in-law, sister-in-law Terri, and I had gone to visit Popsi in some type of facility. My mother-in-law had prepared the most delicious meal, which consisted of collards, or turnip greens, and potatoes. He loved this wonderful food so much, he wanted a second serving. I remember going over to the fridge to get him more greens, but I was having a hard time finding them. The whole time I was looking, Popsi was standing right beside me peering over my shoulder. Later in my dream, he was standing at a counter, talking to a lady who works at the facility, about a private, on-site, two-story condo. She told him that he could purchase the space for $2700—$2800 a month. Popsi started jumping up and down because he was so excited about being able to purchase his own private section. The dream ended with all four of us sitting down at the table with Popsi eating his second helping of greens.

Two days later, I called my mother-in-law and asked her if she had cooked any turnip greens or collards lately. I told her about my dream and she explained that she had been visiting her ninety-nine-year-old mother at the nursing home and her mother was served a lunch of greens and potatoes.

My mother-in-law said her mother would not usually eat greens, but this time she really enjoyed them. While the nurse was feeding her mother the greens, my mother–in-law was looking at the picture of Popsi, which was kept next to her mother's bed. She also paid her mother's rent before leaving. I told her that Popsi knew I would give her the message and this was his way of letting her know that he will always be with her.

TUESDAY NOV. 3, 2009

I DREAMED THAT MY MOTHER IN-LAW TERRi AND MYSELF HAD WENT TO VISIT MY FATHER-IN-LAW IN SOME TYPE OF FACILITY AND MY FATHER IN LAW WAS EATING AND HE WAS EATING COLLARDS OR TURNIP GREENS (PROBABLY) AND HE LOVED THEM SO MUCH HE WANTED MORE OF THEM. I REMEMBER LOOKING IN THE FRIDGE TO SEE IF I COULD FIND POPS, SOME MORE GREENS AND GRAM SAID THERE IS MORE GREENS AND POINTED THEM OUT TO ME. POPSI WAS STANDING BESIDE ME AND WAS TALKING TO A LADY AT THE COUNTER AND WAS TALKING TO HER ABOUT A PRIVATE TWO STORY FACILITY THAT HE COULD PURCHASE AND $2700.00 - 2800.00 ADDitional AMOUNT FOR THE PRIVATE FACILITY CAME TO MY MIND. POPS STARTED JUMPING UP AND DOWN HE WAS SO EXCITED ABOUT HIS OWN PRIVATE SECTION of THE FACILITY. THE NEXT THING I KNEW IS THAT WE'RE AN

FOUR WAS SETTING DOWN AT
THE TABLE W/ POPS, EATING
HIS GREENS.

*** ACTUAL EVENT TO THIS
DREAM ***
NOV. 5TH 2009 THURSDAY
I CALLED MY MOTHER-IN-LAW AND ASKED
IF WE WERE GOING OUT TO DINNER AND
LATER I ASKED HER IF SHE HAD RECENTLY COOKED
TURNIP GREENS OR COLLARDS AND MY MOTHER-IN-LAW
ASKED WHY DO YOU ASK AND I TOLD HER ABOUT MY
DREAM I HAD ABOUT POPS, ABOVE ON THIS PAGE.
MY MOTHER-IN-LAW WENT ON TO SAY THAT
MOTHER SHE WAS VISITING HER MOTHER MAW MAW WHO
IS IN A NURSING HOME AND THEY BROUGHT MAW MAW'S
LUNCH TO HER AND THEY SERVED MAW MAW
GREENS. MY MOTHER IN LAW SAID THAT WHEN THE
NURSE WAS FEEDING MAW MAW SHE WAS LOOKING
AT MY FATHER-IN-LAW'S PICTURE HANGING ON THE WALL.
THE NEXT STRANGE THING WAS THAT MAW MAW
USUALLY WILL NEVER EAT GREENS, BUT THIS TIME
SHE ATE EVERY BITE OF HER GREENS. AND SHE REALLY
ENJOYED THEM. I WENT ON AND TOLD MY MOTHER-IN-LAW
THE REST OF MY DREAM AND SHE SAID SHE HAD
WENT UP TO THE COUNTER TO PAY MAW MAW'S BILL
TO THE NURSING HOME. I TOLD MY MOTHER-IN-LAW
THAT THIS WAS POPSI'S WAY TO LET HER KNOW
HE IS ALWAYS W/ HER AND HE KNEW I WOULD
GIVE HER THE MESSAGE. I TOLD GRAM, THAT POPSI
WAS JUMPING UP AND DOWN W/ JOY AND THAT
HE WAS VERY HAPPY.

MAW MAW,
ALSO HAD FRIED
SLICED POTATOES

CHAPTER NINE

believe

*I*n 2007, I dreamed I was lying on my living room couch, communicating with an angel. The angel showed me a light yellow, wooden plaque with the word "Believe" on it. The angel told me that I didn't believe but should, and I knew this was a message from heaven. I know that I'm supposed to deliver the message that I received that night from my angel.

A couple of weeks after the dream, I went into a store with some friends from work and I saw a wooden plaque with the word "Believe" on it just like the one in my dream. I knew I had to get it for my living room.

In 2008, I started purchasing everything I could find with the word "Believe" on it and giving them as gifts. I was at Wal-Mart and was wishing I could find a box of chocolates with the word "Believe" on it for a friend of mine at work who really loves chocolate. A few minutes later I found myself on the Christmas aisle that had all the Christmas candy, and, sure enough, there was a box of candy wrapped in a beautifully designed red box with the word "Believe" in big gold letters. There were only four boxes on the shelf, so I purchased three. There must have been a reason I left one of the boxes on the shelf. When giving the "Believe" gifts, I share my dream. I know that I'm supposed to share this dream in order to make a difference in other people's lives when they really need something to *believe* in and to confirm there really is a higher power at work.

"Everything is possible for one who believes"

Mark 9:23

"Therefore I tell you, all things whatever you ask for in prayer, believe that you have received it, and it shall be yours."

Mark 11:24

BELIEVE

2007

I DREAMED I WAS LAYING ON MY LIVING ROOM COUCH AND IN THE DREAM I WAS COMMUNICATING WITH AN ANGEL. THE ANGEL SHOWED ME A WOODEN PLAQUE IN LIGHT YELLOW WITH THE WORD BELIEVE ON IT. THE ANGEL TOLD ME THAT I WASN'T BELIEVING AND THAT I HAD TO BELIEVE. THIS DREAM WAS AMAZING, BECAUSE IT REALLY HELPED TO OPEN MY EYES TO A lot OF THINGS THAT WAS GOING ON IN MY life. I KNEW THIS WAS A MESSAGE FROM HEAVEN. I KNOW THAT I'M SUPPOSE TO SHARE THE MESSAGE THAT I RECEIVED FROM MY ANGEL WITH OTHERS TO MAKE A DIFFERENCE IN THEIR lives.

CHAPTER TEN

i visited my mother and family in heaven

October 2003: Through my dreams, I entered the most beautiful and peaceful place I have ever been to. When I arrived in heaven, I cannot even begin to explain how bright and beautiful everything was: from the green grass to the most beautifully colored flowers I have ever seen.

My mother Betty Thacker passed from breast cancer November 26, 1990. The loss of my mother was very difficult for me because my mother and I had such a close and loving relationship. To this day I can still remember laying my head in her lap and she would rub my back. After my mother's death she would let me know she was still around me by running her fingers down my back. My mother was a very caring and loving person.

My grandmother Lucille Jackson passed September 29, 1993 from heart failure. I remember when my grandmother was starting her journey to heaven she looked at me and told me that she loved all of us very much but she was ready to go home and be with God. My grandmother was the best grandmother ever!

My uncle Fred Jackson passed on October 9, 1993, ten days after my grandmother passed away. My uncle Fred was handicapped due to brain damage from high fevers at the age of two. The doctors didn't think he would live past that year. My grandmother and grandfather took care of Fred all of his life. Fred died from a broken heart after my grandmother died because my grandmother did everything for him and he grieved himself to death over the loss of my grandmother. My grandfather found Fred lying in the hallway of their home at the time of his death. Fred is a very loving man with a heart of gold. Our family was very close and was full of love. I can't explain in words how much of a blessing it was for me to visit with them in heaven.

I remember walking alone in total peace, and as I looked ahead, I saw my mother from a distance. I couldn't get to her fast enough. When I reached her, she was beaming and looked so beautiful! My mother was so excited to see me and she wanted to show me where she lived with my grandma and her brother, Fred. As my mother and I walked together in this beautiful place, I loved feeling the bright, beautiful sun beating down on my face. I was so happy to be in her presence, feeling all her love surrounding me.

When we got to my mother's house, she opened the door and I saw my grandma and Fred. It felt so good to be with them again, to feel nothing but peace and love, and to know that they were all together and happy. The house my family lived in was beautiful, peaceful, bright, and sunny. In my dream, I looked over toward a window in an adjacent room and there were the brightest white curtains I have ever seen. I visited with my family for quite some time, and after a while, I knew I had to leave my loving family in heaven and go back home, knowing I could visit with them any time I desired. This dream was a true gift from God.

OCTOBER 2003

I DREAMED I VISITED MY
MOTHER IN HEAVEN.
I REMEMBER EVERYTHING
WAS SO BRIGHT AND BEAUTIFUL.
THERE WERE BEAUTIFUL FLOWERS
EVERY WHERE. I HAD NEVER
~~CRIED~~ FELT SO MUCH LOVE AND
PEACE AT A PLACE BEFORE.
AFTER A FEW MINUTES I LOOKED
UP AND I SAW MY MOTHER IN
A DISTANCE. I WAS SO EXCITED
TO SEE MY MOTHER I COULDN'T
GET TO HER FAST ENOUGH. WHEN
I GOT TO MY MOM WE HUGGED
EACH OTHER AND MY MOTHER
LOOKED SO BEAUTIFUL. MY MOTHER
WAS EXCITED TO SEE ME AND WANTED
TO SHOW ME WHERE HER AND MY
GRANMOTHER AND HER BROTHER FRED
LIVED. AS MY MOTHER AND I WERE
WALKING I COULD FEEL THE BEAUTIFUL
SUN ON MY FACE. I WAS SO HAPPY
TO BE WITH MY MOM AND JUST FEELING

HER LOVE ALL AROUND ME.
WHEN WE ARRIVED AT MY
MOTHER'S HOUSE SHE OPENED
THE DOOR AND I SAW MY GRANDMOTHER
AND FRED. IT FELT SO GOOD TO SEE
THEM AGAIN. AND TO FEEL THEIR
LOVE AND PEACE ALL AROUND US.
THE HOUSE MY FAMILY LIVED IN
WAS BEAUTIFUL, PEACEFUL, BRIGHT AND
SUNNY. IN MY DREAM I LOOKED
OVER TOWARD A WINDOW IN AN
ADJACENT ROOM AND THERE WERE
THE BRIGHTEST WHITE CURTAINS
I HAVE EVER SEEN. I VISITED
WITH MY FAMILY FOR QUITE SOME
TIME AND I KNEW I HAD TO LEAVE
MY LOVING FAMILY IN HEAVEN AND
GO BACK HOME. I KNEW I COULD
VISIT MY FAMILY ANYTIME, THIS
DREAM WAS A TRUE GIFT FROM GOD.

CHAPTER ELEVEN

a devastating storm

*J*uly 2005: I dreamed I was in a bad storm and I saw houses being blown away right before my eyes. In the dream, I was in a house and part of it just came apart. I was rushing to get out before the entire house was destroyed. A few minutes later, I was flying in the air on a boat, looking down at all the destruction on the ground. Later in my dream, I saw newspaper headlines talking about the storm and all the devastation as a result.

A month later, on August 28, 2005, hurricane Katrina hit New Orleans with a devastating effect.

Was it a coincidence? I don't think so because there is no such thing as coincidence.

KATRINA

July 2005

I DREAMED I WAS IN THIS HOUSE
AND THE WEATHER WAS REALLY
BAD OUTSIDE. I LOOKED OUT THE
WINDOW AND SAW TREES FALLING
AND HOUSES BEING DESTROYED.
THEN ALL OF A SUDDEN THE HOUSE
I WAS IN JUST CAME APART AND
I WAS RUSHING TO GET OUT
BEFORE THE ENTIRE HOUSE WAS
DESTROYED. A FEW MINUTES LATER
I WAS FLYING IN THE AIR ON A
BOAT LOOKING DOWN AT ALL THE
DESTRUCTION, ON THE GROUND.
LATER IN MY DREAM I SAW
NEWSPAPER HEADLINES TALKING
ABOUT THE STORM AND ALL THE
DEVASTATION ~~DREAD~~ DUE TO THE
STORM.

A MONTH LATER AUGUST 28, 2005
HURRICANE KATRINA HIT NEW ORLEANS
WITH A DEVASTATING EFFECT.
WAS IT A COINCIDENCE? I DON'T THINK
SO BECAUSE THERE IS NO SUCH THING
AS COINCIDENCE.

CHAPTER TWELVE

december's tornado

*D*ecember 17, 2011: I dreamed that our family was celebrating Christmas and a big storm came out of nowhere. Everyone ran to take cover. My granddaughter Dakota and my husband Brian were with me, and we found shelter in a building that resembled a white cement bridge. I remember looking out and seeing a huge tornado coming in our direction. As the storm was coming toward us, we hovered together. We put Dakota in between us, knowing that it would be the safest place for her and hoping our bodies would protect her from any falling debris. After the tornado passed, we exited the shelter and were amazed at all the destruction. We started walking through the neighborhood and I thought to myself that we were fortunate to be alive.

The next morning, I told Brian about my dream and he said, "This isn't tornado season and we never have tornados in December." I told him that may be the case, but we have severe weather coming our way. We didn't discuss my dream again until December 22, 2011, when bad weather started rolling in and tornado watches and warnings were being issued in our county and surrounding areas. I was at work and I received a text from my husband. He said, "Honey, you might be right about the tornado," and I responded by saying, "I hope it's not going to be as bad as the tornado in my dream."

When I got off from work and started driving home, it was raining so hard I could barely see the road. I got home and Brian asked if I wanted to go out for an early dinner. I knew Brian had been cooped up in the house all day working and needed a break, so I agreed, but the whole time I was thinking to myself that we must be crazy to go out in this weather. On the way back home from dinner, Brian received a phone call from his friend Jim in Rome, Georgia saying that a huge tree had fallen on his three cars, house, boat shed, and boat. Brian asked Jim if he needed him to come up to Rome and help him with anything, but Jim said no. They were okay, just a little shaken up. Brian and I went home, turned on the news, and found out that my hometown, Rome, Georgia, was one of the cities that was hit the worst by the tornado.

A few minutes later on the news, a young couple from Calhoun, Georgia were being interviewed about how they survived the storm (Slone, et al. December

27, 2011). They decided they would put their small child between them and hang on to each other right before the tornado barreled down on their home. The tornado destroyed their home and the force of the storm rolled them into their front yard. As they were rolling, they were holding onto each other. The young couple and their child had only minor cuts and bruises. I was amazed because Brian and I did the same thing with our granddaughter Dakota in my dream. Twenty-three homes and six businesses were destroyed in the tornado in Rome, Georgia. Despite all the destruction, only three minor injuries were reported. The tornado was determined to be an F-2 tornado, which brought winds of around 111–135 miles per hour.

12/19/11 SATURDAY
I DREAM THAT OUR FAMILY WAS
CELEBRATING CHRISTMAS AND THIS BIG
STORM CAME OUT OF NO WHERE. EVERYONE
WAS STARTING TO RUN TO TAKE COVER.

IN MY
JOURNAL
WHEN I
TOLD MY
HUSBAND
ABOUT MY
DREAM
WHEN I
WOKE UP
THE MORNING
OF THE
12/18 I/4.
SAID, THIS
ISN'T
TORNADO
SEASON
AND THUNDERS
IT HAS
NEVER
HAPPENED
IN THE
DECEMBER.

DAKOTA AND BRION WAS W/ME AND
WE FOUND SHELTER IN THIS SHELTER
THAT RESEMBLED A WHITE CEMENT
BRIDGE OR SOMETHING SIMILAR I
REMEMBER LOOKING OUT AND SEEING
THIS HUGE TORNADO COMING IN OUR
DIRECTION AND AS I SAW THE STORMING
COMING TOWARD US WE ALL HOVERED
TOGETHER. AFTER A FEW MINUTES
THE STORM PASSED OVER AND AS
WE EXITED THE PLACE WE TOOK COVER
IN THERE WERE DESTRUCTION EVERYWHERE
WE WERE GOING THROUGH DIFFERENT
AREA'S CHECKING OUT THE DAMAGE
I REMEMBER THINKING WE WERE
VERY FORTUNATE TO BE ALIVE AND
I WAS ALSO SURPRISED THAT WE SURVIVED
THE STORM.

Water

Water represents how we express our
emotions and sentiments.

Water nourishes us so
dreams pertaining to water
most likely are about family or
close loved ones.

The symbol of water can show a journey—
one as simple as a flowing river
with organized emotions
or as stressful as conquering obstacles
as in crossing a river.

Water also represents our memories.

CHAPTER THIRTEEN

handed a key to the church

On October 1, 2008, I dreamed I was at church sitting in a chair in a circle and our reverend, Reverend Padgett, was sitting across the room from me. I went to a table to get some class material and Reverend Padgett came up to me and handed me a key. I had no clue what the key from my dream was for until a few weeks later when I met with Reverend Padgett at the church to discuss the position for a Youth Educational Director. Reverend Padgett asked me what brought me to the church and I explained to him that I felt like I was guided by a number of things, including my psychic friends. I went on to tell Reverend Padgett about my premonition dreams I would have as a small child. He was amazed by my story and interested in developing my gift. I explained that I felt like I would be accepted at the church and members wouldn't think I was crazy or weird. Reverend Padgett asked me if I had any dreams about the church and I told him about the dream with the key. He had a strange look on his face and said, "If you get the Youth Educational Directors position, you will get a key to the church." On the 29th, I was attending a visioning class that Reverend Padgett was hosting and chairs were set up in a circle. Sure enough, I had to go to the table to get material for the class, just like I had dreamed. That night, Reverend Padgett told me the Board of Directors of the church had accepted me as the Youth Director, and that he would be giving me a key to the church.

10/1/08

I DREAMED I WAS AT CHURCH
AND I REMEMBER SITTING IN
CHAIRS IN A CIRCLE AND REVEREND
PADGET WAS SITTING ACROSS THE
ROOM. I WENT UP TO A TABLE
AND FOR WHATEVER REASON
REVEREND PADGET HANDED ME A
KEY. I'M NOT SURE WHAT THE
KEY WAS FOR.

ACTUAL EVENT THAT TOOK
PLACE THAT REGARDING MY
DREAM RECORDED IN THIS BOOK
FOR THE DATE 10/1/08

IN MY DREAM REVEREND
PADGETT HANDED ME A KEY
WHICH I DIDN'T UNDERSTAND
UNTIL 10/22 UNTIL I MEET
W/ REVEREND PADGETT REGARDING
A POSITION OF YOUTH EDUCATIONAL
DIRECTOR. IT WAS FUNNY BECAUSE
WHEN I WAS DISCUSSING THE POSITION
W/ REVEREND PADGETT HE ASKED
ME WHAT BROUGHT ME TO THE UNIT-
CHURCH AND I EXPLAINED TO HIM
I WAS GUIDED TO THE CHURCH
BY ALL MY PSYCHIC FRIENDS,
BECAUSE ALL MY LIFE I WOULD
HAVE DREAMS AND THAT
WOULD COME TRUE AND MY FRIENDS
TOLD ME, I SHOULD GO TO A UNITY
CHURCH, BECAUSE PEOPLE WOULDN'T
THINK I WAS CRAZY.

I could tell that Reverend Padgett was amazed by my story. Reverend Padgett asked me what I was doing to help develope my gift more and I told him, I was meditating. Reverend Padgett asked me if I had any dreams about the church and I said, that I had dreamed I was in a meeting w/him and he handed me a key and he had a strange look on his face. He looked at me and said, if I got the position I would get a key to the church.

10/29/08 I attended the visioning class and we discussed the educational director position and Reverend Padgett wanted me to take the lead position of the director and told me, he would be getting me a key. It's strange because Suzanna Alexandria was also interested in the position if there was going to be compensation for the position. Shortly after I applied for the position the board decided →

TO NOT MAKE THE position A <u>DIRECTOR</u> PAID position. REVEREND PADGETT ASKED ME IF THAT WOULD MAKE A DIFFERENCE TO ME. AND I TOLD HIM NO, BECAUSE I WAS WANTING THE position TO HELP ME GET OUT OF THE BOX AND TO MAKE ME GROW MORE SPIRITUALLY AND BECAUSE I DO love KIDS.

ORIGINALLY I TOLD REVEREND PADGETT THAT IF I KNEW THAT SUZANNA HAD APPLIED FOR THE position I PROBABLY WOULDN'T HAVE APPLIED BECAUSE SUZANNA HAD BEEN W/ THE CHURCH A lot LONGER THAN ME AND SHE REALly loves THE CHILDREN AND HAS A lot OF GREAT IDEA'S FOR THE position.

THE POINT I'M TRYING TO MAKE IS THAT I WAS MEANT TO HAVE THE position AND GOD AND THE UNIVERSE

DELIVERED THE position TO ME.

REVEREND PADGETT WANTS ME
TO HAVE SUZANNA TO HANDLE
THE INFANTS & TODDLER CLASS
AND ME TO HANDLE EVERYTHING
ELSE. SUZANNA IS ALREADY IN
CHARGE OF HANDLING THE
TODDLER CLASSES.

ACTUAL EVENT → 11/12/08 REVEREND PADGETT GAVE ME THE
KEY TO THE CHURCH

CHAPTER FOURTEEN

a spirit of a police officer is protecting my home

On January 30, 2010, I dreamed that I was hanging clothes in my laundry room, and all of a sudden, I looked to my left toward the garage door and it opened. Right away I knew it was a spirit. I walked over and shut the door, waiting a few minutes to see if the spirit would open the door again, but it stayed closed.

The next day, I was in the laundry room hanging up clothes and the light started flickering. It then went off completely, so I started trying the light switch to see if the light would come back on; nothing happened. I called to my husband in the living room and told him he needed to replace the bulb. He was busy doing something at the time, but he promised he would get to it as soon as he was done. Later that evening, I went back in the laundry room and the light came on without any problem. After getting the clothes, I asked my husband if he had changed the bulb, but he said he had forgotten about it. Right away I thought about the dream I'd had the night before and knew the spirit from my dream was trying to get my attention; that it had a message for me.

Four days later, I called Mary Occhino on her show and asked her about the spirit and why it was trying to contact me. Mary asked me to put up a small video camera with motion sensors and an EVP voice recorder to see what is going on when I'm not at home. She felt that the garage door must be opening and closing whenever we were away from the house. Mary then went on to say that the spirit had been a police officer when he was in the physical. He was trying to tell us to make sure all the windows and doors were secure. Mary described a man in his twenties whom she felt had been trying to get in the house through a window, but wasn't yet able to. I told her I had been getting uneasy feelings lately about someone messing around our house and had been telling my son Jordan to make sure he set the security system before going to bed. I had also started locking the door leading out to the garage when I left for work in the morning, as well as pushing the lock button on my car door as soon as I got in the car because of my uneasy feeling.

To this day, the light bulb still hasn't been replaced in my laundry room and is still working. I still haven't set up the video cameras in my home, but one day I might, just to validate different things that take place in my house.

SPIRIT PROTECTING

1/30/10 SATURDAY

I WAS ASLEEP AND I THINK I WAS DREAMING THIS, BUT MAYBE I WASN'T SLEEPING. I WAS DREAMING THAT THE COVERS ON MY BED WAS BEING PULLED VERY SLOWLY. I REMEMBER I WAS WOKEN UP FROM THE DREAM AND I LOOKED OVER AT THE CLOCK AND THE TIME WAS 3:16 AM WHICH IS A little BEFORE 3:00 BY OUR CLOCK BECAUSE OUR CLOCK IS SET AHEAD BY 20 MINUTES. I REMEMBER THINKING I NEEDED TO WAKE BRIAN UP AND ASKED HIM, HE HAD FELT ANYTHING.

LATER I DREAMED I WAS IN THE LAUNDRY ROOM HANGING UP CLOTHES AND I LOOKED TO THE RIGHT OF ME AND NOTICED THE DOOR LEADING OUT TO THE GARAGE WAS OPENED AND I KNEW THE DOOR WAS OPENED BY A SPIRIT. I WALKED OVER TO THE DOOR AND SHUT IT AND I THOUGHT I WILL SEE IF THE DOOR OPENS ON

SPIRIT PROTECTING
1/31/10 SUNDAY
it OWN AGAIN.

1/31/10 10:20 PM.

** ACTUAL EVENT THAT TOOK PLACE IN MY LIVING ROOM ON SUNDAY 1/31/10. I WAS SITTING WATCHING GHOST WHISPER AND ALL OF A SUDDEN I FELT A COLD CHILL TO THE BACK OF MY NECK AND MY HEAD STARTED FEELING A TINGLEY FEELING — ANOTHER WAY TO EXPLAIN THE FEELING IS LIKE A STATIC ELECTRICITY ELECTRICAL STATIC FEELING AS IF SOMEONE WAS MESSING W/ MY HAIR, SO I REACHED UP AND PUT MY HANDS UP TO THE TOP OF MY HEAD. ***

CHAPTER FIFTEEN

a message from my brother-in-law's father

ebruary 25, 2010: We arrived in Chicago for my son's martial arts seminar and were staying with my husband's sister Carla and her husband Bob. My brother-in–law's birthday was the next day, so we were excited about being in Chicago in order to celebrate with him. That night, I dreamed that my son, Jordan, came to me and said, "Mom, did you see that apparition over there?" I looked but didn't see anything. A few minutes later, he pointed to the door and right away I knew it was my brother-in-law's father. Bob's father had thinning hair and the same physique as his son. I rushed over to the door, took his hand, and told him how happy we were to see him and we loved him. He sat down at a table and I sat across from him. He started hitting his hand softly on the table and said, "You need to drink more water." Bob's father and I chatted for a few more minutes and again, I told him we loved him. I turned around and he was gone, but Jordan said, "Mom, there he is over there eating cake." I looked where Jordan was pointing and saw him standing in Bob's family room, cutting a huge piece of cake, putting it in his mouth, and just smiling. You could tell he was really enjoying the cake. I woke up from the dream around three o'clock in the morning, and I couldn't go back to sleep because I knew I had a birthday message for Bob from his dad. I kept lying in the bed, thinking about how I was going to give Bob the message from his dad. I never know how people will perceive these types of messages and really didn't know if Bob believed in my gift. I finally decided that I would have been doing him a disservice by not relaying the birthday message. So, I thought the right time to deliver the message would present itself.

The next morning, my son Jordan and his girlfriend wanted to go snowboarding, so we got up, got dressed, and made plans. We agreed that Carla would take us to the snowboarding place and Bob would meet up with us a little later. When Bob showed up, we were sitting, watching the kids on the slopes, and talking. I thought this was the time I needed to give Bob the message, so I proceeded to tell him about my dream. I went on to tell Bob that his dad wanted him to know that he was going to be with him on his birthday. Carla told me that Bob and his dad had been best friends; they were very close and loved spending time together. Bob said that his father was a real health nut toward the end of his life, always making health drinks. He really tried watching what he ate because of his health. He loved sweets, but couldn't eat them because of his health problems. I told Bob his dad doesn't have to worry about what he eats now; he is eating all the cake he wants in heaven. I was so happy to be able to give him the birthday message from his dad. There is no greater experience than being able to communicate with spirits and to deliver messages to their loved ones here on earth. Remember, there is no death, life is eternal.

⟨①

2/25/10 Thursday
My family and I were in
Chicago for Jordan's choir seminar
and my brother in laws birthday
is on 2/26/10.

In my dream my son Jordan
came to me, saying he saw a spirit
and I asked him where and as he was
about to tell me and he pointed to
the front door and said there he is
so I walked to the front door to talk
to the spirit and I reached for his
hand and told him I was glad to see
him and told him we loved him.
The spirit was balding and had very little
hair the spirit came into the house
and sat down and we were talking
and he the spirit was hitting his hand
on the table sideways and he said, you
need to drink more water and he was
talking about the daily allowances of
Water which is 6-8 glasses a day.
I told the spirit we loved him and
I knew the spirit he was my Mother's

②

2/25/10 Thursday

in law father, because he had the same
body figure as my mother in law. After
a few minutes the spirit got up and
walked into another room and my
son Jordan said mom look at the
spirit and I looked into the other
room and saw the spirit getting himself
a large piece of cake and I watched
him put a piece of cake up to his
mouth and I could tell he was really
enjoying the cake at that moment I
knew that the message was for my
brother in law, that he dad would be
with him on his birthday. This dream
woke me up and I couldn't go back
to sleep because I couldn't get the
spirit off my mind.

ACTUAL EVENT 2/26/10
WE HAD TAKEN JORDAN AND HANNAH
SNOWBOARDING AND AS WE WERE TALKING
I TURNED TO MY BROTHER-IN-LAW AND
TOLD HIM, HIS FATHER VISITED ME
LAST NIGHT AND I PROCEEDED TO TELL
HIM ABOUT MY DREAM AND HE SAID,

(3)

2/25/10 Thursday

HE WANTED TO HEAR ALL ABOUT IT.
I PROCEEDED TO TELL HIM ABOUT MY
DREAM AND I DESCRIBED HIS DAD'S
APPEARANCE TO MY BROTHER-IN-LAW.
MY BROTHER-IN-LAW AND SISTER
IN LAW WENT ON TO SAY BEFORE
HIS FATHER DIED HE HAD BECAME A
REAL HEALTH NUT AND HE WOULD
PREPARE CERTAIN HEALTH DRINKS. USING
A BLENDER. HE WOULD LECTURE EVERYBODY
ABOUT SODIUM BECAUSE HE HAD PROBLEMS
W/ HIS HEART. BOB & CARLA SAID HE
LOVED CAKES BUT COULDN'T HAVE
CAKE BEFORE HE PASSED BECAUSE
OF HEALTH ISSUES.

CHAPTER SIXTEEN

a promise to granddaddy

*I*n January 2008, my granddaddy was starting his journey to heaven and laying in his hospital bed in a coma. I leaned over him and said, "Granddaddy, I know you don't understand how I know certain things are going to happen before they actually take place, but one day you will." At that moment, I promised my granddaddy that after he got to heaven, either I would go to him or he would come to me.

A few months after my Granddaddy's passing, I had a dream that he was lying in the bed and we were having a conversation. He looked up at me and asked, "Rhonda, is it really you?" I answered, "Yes Granddaddy, it's me." At that moment, he got up from his bed and stood directly in front of me. As he started to walk toward me, I felt his spirit as it passed through my body. It woke me up out of a sound sleep. I knew then that my granddaddy heard my promise to him as he lay in his hospital bed. Now I know that he understands the special gift that God has given me. To this day, my granddaddy and I continue to enjoy each other's visits.

4:45 8/4/08

I DREAMED I WAS GOING TO
THIS PLACE THAT MY GRANDADDY
OWNED TO GET ICE. WHEN I GOT TO
THE PLACE PEOPLE ASKED IF MY
GRANDADDY (ANOTHER NAME) KNEW I WAS GETTING
THE ICE AND I SAID OF COURSE
IT WAS IF THEY DIDN'T KNOW I
WAS HIS GRANDAUGHTER. THEY WERE
CALLING MY GRANDADDY A NAME, BUT
I CAN'T REMEMBER THE NAME RIGHT
OFF. IN MY DREAM MY GRANDADDY
WAS A WEALTHY MAN AND WAS
VERY WELL KNOW BY EVERYONE. I
REMEMBER A LOT OF PEOPLE WAS SITTING
ON A BED AND MY GRANDADDY TOLD
A MAN THAT THERE WAS SOMEONE ON
THE BED WAS EVIL OR SOMETHING TO
THAT EFFECT AND THEN SOMEONE POINTED
AT ME AND IT SEEMED MY NAME WAS
BRENDA AT THAT POINT AND THE MAN
SAID NOT HER AT THAT POINT I FELT
THE MAN KNEW I WAS THE GRANDAUGHTER.
MY GRANDADDY WAS LAYING ON THE BED
ACROSS THE ROOM, SO I GOT UP AND WALKED

OVER TO MY GRANDADDY AND SAT
BESIDE HIM AND I SAID GRANDADDY
I'M HERE IT'S RHONDA AND MY
GRANDADDY SAID, IS ILLS THAT YOU AND
ALL OF A SUDDEN MY GRANDADDY PASSED
AWAY AND ALL OF A SUDDEN MY
GRANDADDY WAS STANDING UP AND
HIS SPIRIT WENT RIGHT THROUGH ME.
I CAN'T DESCRIBE THE FEELING THAT
I EXPERIENCED AFTER HIS SPIRIT WENT
THROUGH ME. I WOKE UP AFTER
THAT.

Fire

Fire symbolizes enthusiasm,
passion and energy.
Think warmth, comfort, romance
and sentimental thoughts.

Fire can represent negative forces
such as destruction, at the same time it can
show a birth of the new.

The amount of control you have in your
dream will tell how much control you have
in specific situations—if the fire is in control
and manageable, you may have similar
situations in your life.

If the fire is spreading and uncontrollably,
you may have lost control
of a certain aspect of your life.

CHAPTER SEVENTEEN

intruder in my apartment

*I*n 1974, I started having dreams of someone breaking into my apartment. Each time I would wake up really scared because they were so real. My mother and sister decided to go to Rome, Georgia and were going to stay overnight to visit with my grandparents. My mother kept asking me if I was going to be okay staying at home all by myself, and I kept reassuring her that I would be fine. That evening, my boyfriend Brian and I went to dinner, came back to my apartment, and hung out for a little while. After Brian left, I got ready for bed and started having an uneasy feeling about staying by myself. I decided I would leave the living room and kitchen lights on in an effort to make myself feel more secure. I figured if someone tried to break in, I would wake up right away because I'm such a light sleeper.

Once I went to bed, all I was thinking about was the dreams I'd had of someone breaking into my apartment. Several hours went by and I found myself watching the clock, thinking that I needed to get some sleep. Finally my eyes got so tired, I found myself drifting off to sleep. In the middle of the night, I was awakened by what sounded like people arguing outside. I remembered looking at the clock; it was two o'clock in the morning. I kept listening to the voices to see if I could recognize any of them. It sounded like some friends who lived in the apartment building next to ours, which made me feel a little more secure knowing that friends were outside. My thought was to get up and see what was going on, but due to the lack of sleep, I dozed off again.

The next morning, my alarm went off and I got up as usual, still feeling pretty tired from the night before. I noticed my bedroom door was cracked, but I knew I'd left the door open so I could see the light in the living room. I got up and walked to my mother's bedroom and had the shock of my life. All the dresser drawers were wide open and a lot of the clothes were scattered on the floor. I went to the kitchen and noticed the sliding glass door was ajar. I ran to my friend's apartment across the hall. I remember banging on her door and my legs were shaking so badly I thought I was going to collapse. My friend came to the door and immediately called the police while her husband searched my apartment. While I was waiting for the police to arrive, I called my mother in Rome and told her what had happened. She got very upset, saying she knew she shouldn't have left me at home alone because she'd had an uneasy feeling about leaving me all by myself. I've always felt that I got my intuition from my mother, but she's never tried to develop it as I have. Once the police arrived, I went back to the apartment and realized that my purse was dumped out on the couch in the living room. All I could think of was what could have happened if I had woken up during the robbery. I'm such a light sleeper, so I couldn't believe I'd slept through the whole event without waking up. After the robbery, it took me years before I could stay home at night by myself. To this day, I feel like my father was there watching over me to make sure I stayed asleep so no harm would come to me. I kept thinking of the dreams I've had of my father; he would be standing outside my bedroom window, telling me he would always be there to protect me.

1974
I dreamed that someone broke
into my apartment Several times
and each time I was so scared
in my dreams It would Wake me
up from a sound sleep.

CHAPTER EIGHTEEN

death of a friend

On June 25, 2008 I dreamed that I came upon a house, which appeared to be a brick, one-story home on a corner lot. If you were looking at the house from the road, there was wooden lattice work, a driveway, and a swimming pool on the right side. It had a nicely landscaped yard with a brick wall along the front where people would sit at family gatherings. The vision of this house bothered me so much that it was the first picture I ever drew in my dream journal.

I noticed in my dream there was a woman, two daughters, and a son lined up in front of the home, and I was assigning numbers to them. I saw a little boy sitting to the side of the home and I went over to him, asking why he was sitting all by himself. He just shrugged his shoulders as if he didn't know what to say, so I lined him up as well and gave him a number. I lined up the mother first, one daughter, one son, the other daughter, and the other son. To this day, I don't know why I was assigning numbers to everyone, but the numbers that kept coming to mind were forty-six and forty-eight.

Later in my dream, I realized that the woman and the children had been killed in the home. I remembered thinking it looked familiar and I must have passed this house before on holidays. They all would be outside with other family members, having cookouts and enjoying each other's company. The husband appeared not to have been home at the time of the murders. I wondered how a husband, and the father of these children, could continue on with his life, enduring the loneliness and sadness.

I was out for a walk with a friend on July 4, 2008 when my cell phone rang. It was my manager at work. I knew if she was calling me on a Saturday, something was definitely wrong. My manager told me that a coworker had a freak accident in her home and had passed away. She had been upstairs at home and fell back into the stair railing, landing on the floor below. Although she got up and initially appeared to be okay, she started having problems and later died at the hospital.

I was very bothered about the death of my coworker because of the dream I'd had about the death of a woman. My coworker had two teenage sons, who I knew were going to be lost without their mother.

At the funeral home, we paid our respects to our coworker's husband and two sons. One of the sons was acting very distant, as if he didn't really know what to do, and was just keeping to himself. It reminded me so much of the young boy in my dream. Everyone was concerned what affect the death of his mother would have on him. As we approached the casket, several of us noticed the swelling and bruising to her face, and it was hard for us to believe that she ever got up from the floor without any help. As I walked by the casket, I was looking at the pictures and there was one of my coworker's house. I was shocked; the house looked just like the one I had drawn in my dream journal.

I would be lying if I said that her death still doesn't bother me to this day, but in order for me to move forward with my life, I had to put her death behind me. Before her death, my coworker was part of our group of ladies from work that would play cards on our lunch break. The first card game we played after her death was in her honor. We laughed and talked to our friend in heaven, and I'm sure she was right there with us in spirit. To this day, we still talk about our friend and know that she is in the presence of God and the angels in heaven.

6/25/08

I ALSO DREAMED THAT I
CAME UPON THIS HOUSE, WHICH
WAS A PRETTY NICE HOUSE.
IT APPEARED TO BE BRICK
AND HAD A NICE YARD.
THEN ALL OF A SUDDEN
THERE WAS A WOMAN, TWO
DAUGHTERS AND A SON LINED
UP IN FRONT OF THE HOME AND
I WAS ASSIGNING NUMBERS
TO THEM AND AS I WAS
ASSIGNING NUMBERS TO THEM
I NOTICED ANOTHER little
BOY SITTING TO THE SIDE OF
THE HOME AND LINED him
UP AS WELL AND GAVE him A
NUMBER. I DON'T KNOW
WHY I WAS ASSIGNING NUMBERS

AND THEN ALL IT A SUDDEN
I REALIZED THAT THE WOMAN
AND THE CHILDREN HAD BEEN
KILLED IN THE HOUSE.
I REMEMBER THINKING
I HAD BEEN PAST THIS
HOUSE BEFORE ON CERTAIN
HOLIDAYS AND ALL OF THEM
WOULD BE OUTSIDE W/ OTHER
FAMILY MEMBERS HAVING
A COOK OUT AND JUST ENJOYING
EACH OTHERS COMPANY.
THE HUSBAND APPEARED NOT
TO HAVE BEEN HOME AT THE
TIME OF THE MURDERS.
ALL I COULD THINK OF WAS
HOW THIS HUSBAND & FATHER
WOULD CONTINUE ON W/ HIS LIFE
AND THE LONELINESS AND
SADNESS THAT HE WAS GOING TO
HAVE TO ENDURE. PLEASE OF PAGE →

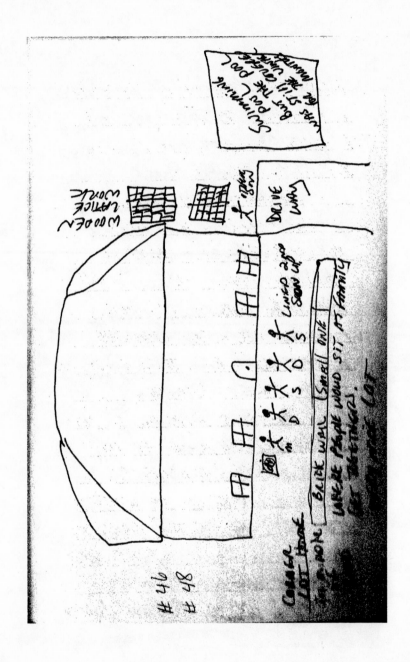

CHAPTER NINETEEN

*a coworker was in trouble and
had negative energy around her*

I dreamed I was attending a funeral for a man at work on November 22, 2008. The whole office was at the funeral home sitting around the casket when the man in the casket opened his eyes. People started running over to him, hugging him. The next thing I knew, the man was out of the casket and standing next to me. I wasn't going to hug him because I felt that everyone was smothering him. I didn't want to do the same thing so I started to walk away, but he reached out and hugged me. The next thing I remember, I was walking out of the funeral home and I told the people that his spirit hadn't passed over yet. The people walking with me didn't quite understand what I was talking about. Donna, one of my coworkers, was walking with me. We were headed to a restaurant and I mentioned we could sit together. When I got there, I was looking for Donna to sit with her, but when I finally found her, we were walking out in the parking lot. The wind was blowing very hard and I felt this evil presence reach and grab my leg. I told Donna we needed to hurry and get in the car. A few minutes later, I went back to the funeral home and walked up to the casket. Now Donna was in the casket and she started moving as if she was very agitated. After waking up from the dream, all I could think about was warning Donna about my dream and telling her to be careful. I knew that her ex-boyfriend had been stalking her and he had been very violent in the past. I couldn't get Donna off my mind the entire weekend.

Two days later, I went in to work and was still looking for Donna. She was nowhere to be found since I'd had my dream, so I started asking people if they knew where Donna was. I was about to approach the receptionist to ask if she'd seen Donna, but then I finally saw her coming down the hallway. I asked her where she had been and Donna said she'd had a doctor's appointment. I told her I needed to talk to her about a dream I had and that I was really concerned.

I explained the dream and told her I felt like there was a negative energy around her. Donna proceeded to tell me that the way I saw her in my dream is the way she had been feeling. She said that during her doctor's appointment, she had even made a remark to her doctor that maybe she was dead and just didn't know it.

Donna also told me that she had been trying to figure out what to do about a new relationship because something was making her feel uneasy about it. She'd been especially agitated over the weekend when I had the dream. I warned her that I felt like there was a negative energy around her and that she needed to surround herself with the white light of Christ for protection. I told Donna to never let her guard down and again expressed how concerned I was about her.

The next Wednesday morning, when I was walking into the office, another coworker, Lisa, pulled up to tell me that something grabbed her right leg in the middle of the night, waking her up out of a sound sleep. Lisa said she was really scared and sat up in the bed, but the spirit grabbed her leg really hard again and she couldn't move. I could see the fear in Lisa's face and it looked as if she was going to cry. She told me she was too scared to stay in her condo because drawers would just open and close in her bathroom.

She told me it usually takes a lot to wake her up from a sound sleep and asked me what I thought. I told her about the dream where a spirit grabbed my right leg and explained that I wasn't only picking up on Donna's energy in my dream, but I was also picking up on her energy as well. I told her she needed to surround herself with the white light of Christ and ask God and the angels to protect her from the negative energy. She could get rid of the spirit by saying, "Be gone, be gone, be gone," telling it to go toward the white light, burning sage, and spraying kosher salt. I told Lisa that Donna and I could go with her at lunch to cleanse her condo to get rid of the spirit. I also asked her if she wanted me to call my friend Mary Occhino, a psychic-medium/intuitive explorer of consciousness. Mary could give her information about the spirit and could advise her on how to get rid of it, which might put her mind at ease.

When we called Mary, Lisa started explaining what was going on in her condo. Mary told her that the spirit was evil, was a thief, and had robbed and later murdered someone. She went on to say that the man wasn't a demon himself, but he could bring in a demon. Lisa asked Mary what she could do to get rid of the spirit and Mary told her to perform the same ritual I had recommended. After speaking with Mary, I told Lisa we could go buy everything we needed at the metaphysical store during lunch and then cleanse her condo of the spirit.

When I got to Donna's office, she was on the phone and was visibly upset. She told me that her son had just hit his father and was arrested for family violence. Donna looked at me and said, "Rhonda, everything you said is happening." I explained what was going on with Lisa, and Donna agreed to go with us to cleanse Lisa's condo. We went to the metaphysical store to get all of our supplies on our lunch hour and headed to Lisa's.

When we arrived, we held hands and I said a prayer for God to circle us with the white light, protecting us from any negative energy. When we finally entered the condo, we started the process of getting everything ready to clear the negative energy. I started getting a tightness in my chest from picking up on the energy of the spirit. I began burning the white sage and saying, "Be gone, be gone, be gone, in the name of the Holy Spirit. Go toward the white light, we are here in love and peace." Donna was spraying the sea salt and Lisa was carrying the incense. It took us the better part of an hour to cleanse the entire condo, and after, there was a big difference in the energy. Before we left, we held hands again and I said another prayer for God to bless the condo and Lisa. I explained to Lisa that she really had to believe that the spirit was gone; if not, it would open the door up for the spirit to come back in to her condo. After the cleansing of the condo, we all could feel the difference in the energy of the condo.

11/22/08 5:00 AM FORWARD

I DREAMED THAT I WAS ATTENDING A FUNERAL FOR A MAN AT WORK. THE WHOLE OFFICE WAS ATTENDING THE FUNERAL. WE WERE AT THE FUNERAL HOME SITTING AROUND THE CASKET AND THE MAN IN THE CASKET OPEN HIS EYES AND EVERYONE WAS TAKEN BY SURPRISE. PEOPLE STARTED RUNNING OVER TO HIM AND STARTED HUGGING HIM. THE NEXT THING I KNOW THE MAN IS STANDING OUT OF THE CASKET AND WAS STANDING NEXT TO ME AND I WASN'T GOING TO GO UP TO HIM AND HUG HIM BECAUSE I FELT THAT EVERYONE WAS SMOTHERING HIM AND I DIDN'T WANT TO DO THAT SO I STARTED TO WALK AWAY AND THE MAN REACHED OVER ME AND HUGGED ME. THE NEXT THING I REMEMBERED IS WE WERE WALKING OUT OF THE FUNERAL HOME AND I TOLD THE PEOPLE HIS SPIRIT HASN'T PAST OVER YET. →

11/22/08 CONTINUED

THE PEOPLE WALKING W/ME DIDN'T
QUITE UNDERSTAND WHAT I WAS TALKING
ABOUT REGARDING HIS SPIRIT. DONNA
HUGHES WAS ONE OF THE PEOPLE
WALKING W/ME AND WE WERE HEADED
TO A RESTAURANT ARE SOMETHING AND
I TOLD DONNA WE COULD SIT TOGETHER
AT THE RESTAURANT. WHEN I GOT
TO THE RESTAURANT I WAS LOOKING
FOR DONNA TO SIT W/HER I FINALLY
FOUND DONNA AND THE NEXT THING
I KNOW WE ARE WALKING OUT IN
A PARKING LOT AND THE WIND WAS
BLOWING HARD AND I FELT THIS EVIL
PRESENTS REACH AND GRAB MY LEG
AND I TOLD DONNA WE NEEDED TO
HURRY AND GET IN THE CAR.
THE NEXT THING I REMEMBER IS
I'M STANDING IN THE A FUNERAL HOME
AND I SEE DONNA IN THE CASKET
AND SHE STARTED MOVING AS IF SHE
WAS VERY AGITATED AND I WAS THINKING
EVEN THOUGH SHE HAD BEEN EMBALMED SHE
WAS STILL REALLY BOTHERED BY SOMETHING ⟶

~~In my dream~~ I woke up right after that. I never knew who the man was. All I know is the spirits never crossed over because something was bothering them and things in their lk ~~were~~ unfinished. Our whole office was really affected by these loses.

11/24/08 I will warn Donna to be careful because she has a old boyfriend who has been stalking here and could be dangerous. However I want share my dream w/her. Hopefully if her boyfriend has any thoughts about harming her I can help stop ~~any~~ future incidents.

CHAPTER TWENTY

civil war soldiers in the shower

*J*uly 31, 2009: I dreamed that I was at my co-worker Lisa's home and there was something going on with her shower. The next thing I knew, I was standing in Lisa's shower and all these different spirits started coming through. It was as if I was directing the spirits to where they needed to go. I knew one of the spirits was a Civil War soldier because of his blue uniform and the long gun he had hanging over his right shoulder. This particular soldier was talking to me for quite some time before I pointed to show him what direction he needed to take. When I woke up the next morning, I kept thinking to myself that I needed to speak to Lisa about the dream. I knew there was a personal message that I needed to give her and that it had something to do with the soldier.

Days passed, and on August 6, 2009, I finally asked Lisa about her shower. She said that she had been dreaming of hearing shower water running during the night, and at three o'clock in the morning, she heard something fall in her shower, waking her up. When Lisa was awoken by the noise, she wondered who could be taking a shower at that time of the night.

I explained to Lisa about my dream and about my giving the spirits in her shower directions, as if they were lost and they didn't know where to go. I told her about the man in the Civil War uniform and that I spoke with him for quite some time. I felt that I needed to give her a message from him. Lisa then began to tell me that she had been lighting a candle at night for Tom, her ex-boyfriend who had died a couple of months earlier. Though Lisa really didn't know the reason for Tom's passing, it had always bothered her. She went on to say that Tom's family wasn't religious and she was worried that Tom was lost. She had been talking to Tom, telling him to go to the white light and that he would be accepted and loved there. I told her that Tom heard her prayers when she talked to him. This was his way of letting her know that he made it home and was safe. Lisa's eyes started to tear up and she knew Tom was finally at rest.

FRIDAY July 31, 2009
I DREAMED THAT I WAS W/ THIS CO-WORKER lisa Campbell AT HER HOME AND THERE WAS SomETHING GOING ON ABOUT HER SHOWER. THE NEXT THING I KNOW JT WAS AS IF I WAS STANDING IN THIS PRETTY GOOD SiZE SHOWER, WHICH I THINK WAS lISA'S AND All OF A SUDDEN All OF THESE DiFFERENT Spirits STARTED COMING THRU HER SHOWER AND IT WAS IF I WAS DiRECTING THE SPIRITS AS TO WHERE THEY NEEDED TO GO. I KNEW THAT ONE SPIRIT WAS lIKE A SoilDERS LiKE From THE So CiViL WAR W/ A GUN HANGING OVER HIS SHoulDER AND HE HAD A BLUE UNiFoRM ON.

CHAPTER TWENTY-ONE

norway bombing and massacre

*M*ay 7, 2011 I dreamed of a high rise building shaking due to a terrorist attack. After the bombing, I was observing all the damage and commotion going on around me. People were scurrying everywhere. A couple of minutes later, I saw a man that I knew was responsible for the bombing and I knew the authorities were frantically looking for him.

Later in the dream, I was at a location where a lot of kids were and I knew that a man was coming to kill them. I started rushing to where the kids were sleeping, trying to get them out of their beds, dressed, and moved to a safe location. I was thinking, if I could get the kids moved fast enough,

I could arrange the beds so the gunman would think the kids were still asleep and they would be safe. A few minutes had passed and I knew the gunman would be there at any moment, so I started getting stressed out and panicked because I couldn't get the kids moved fast enough. It was at that moment in my dream that I knew I wasn't going to be able to save them. I was so disturbed by the dream. It woke me up and I couldn't get the kids out of my mind. The next morning, I discussed the dream with my husband and I told him that it was one dream I hoped never came true.

May 9,2011: I was still really bothered by the dreams I'd had over the weekend and decided to share them with my good friend, Mary Occhino. I hoped this would help me release some of the anxiety I was feeling from my dream and to validate any future events. The dreams from the weekend were so detailed and vivid; I kept playing them out in my mind's eye.

On July 22, 2011, I arrived home from work and my husband asked me if I'd heard about the kids who were attacked in Norway, but I hadn't. Right away, I started getting this sick feeling in the pit of my stomach. I turned on the TV to get more information about the shootings. The news was reporting that Anders Behrin Breivik had set off a bomb in the capital of Oslo that killed seven people just before driving to a camp to kill the kids (Ritter July 23, 2011). All I could think of after the event was that if I'd had a few more details in my dream, maybe I could have warned the government and saved the lives of the victims.

I'm not sure why I'm shown the things that I see when I'm asleep, but I know that a higher power is at work. I take comfort in knowing that God is in control and I know there is a reason for everything.

FIRE

From: Rhonda Leiva [bettyhowardthacker@yahoo.com]
Sent: July 26, 2011 7:52 PM
To: Leiva, Rhonda
Subject: Fw: Dream

--- On Mon, 5/9/11, Rhonda Leiva *<bettyhowardthacker@yahoo.com>* wrote:

From: Rhonda Leiva <bettyhowardthacker@yahoo.com>
Subject: Dream
To: maryocchino@yahoo.com
Date: Monday, May 9, 2011, 9:33 AM

Hi Mary,

I just wanted to share my dreams with you from the past couple of nights. It makes me feel better to just share them with somebody who can help validate them for me.

Saturday night, I had a dream about a high rise building a shaking and there was also something to do with a subway and I felt like it had something to do with terrorist. *— NORWAY*

Last night, I dreamed that we were being bombed or something and things were falling from the sky and I was running and taking cover to keep the falling debri from hitting me. The strangest thing when I looked up in the sky there were seals or dolphins crashing down and next there was a helicopter crashing from the sky. *NAVY Seals CRASH*

The next thing I know I'm where these kids are and I know that someone is coming to kill them so I'm trying to get them dressed and out of their beds so I can move them to another location and fix their beds so the men that are coming will think the kids are there but in fact be in a different location. In my dream I'm stressing because I couldn't get the kids moved fast enough. *— NORWAY*

Love You More,
Rhonda

CHAPTER TWENTY-TWO

navy seals crash

*M*ay 8, 2011: I dreamed we were being bombed. Things were falling from the sky and I was running to take cover to keep the falling debris from hitting me. The strangest thing was that when I looked up in the sky, I saw seals or dolphins crashing down. Then, to the right of me, a helicopter came crashing down from the sky.

Little did I know, my dream would come true on August 6, 2011. Insurgents shot down a United States military helicopter while fighting in Eastern Afghanistan, killing thirty Americans who came from the Navy, Air Force, and Army: most of them Navy Seals from Team Six (CBS News August 6, 2011).

Between the Norway Killings and the Navy Seals crash, it really took a toll on me, both mentally and emotionally.

From: Rhonda Leiva [bettyhowardthacker@yahoo.com]
Sent: July 26, 2011 7:52 PM
To: Leiva, Rhonda
Subject: Fw: Dream

--- On Mon, 5/9/11, Rhonda Leiva <*bettyhowardthacker@yahoo.com*> wrote:

From: Rhonda Leiva <bettyhowardthacker@yahoo.com>
Subject: Dream
To: maryocchino@yahoo.com
Date: Monday, May 9, 2011, 9:33 AM

Hi Mary,

I just wanted to share my dreams with you from the past couple of nights. It makes me
feel better to just share them with somebody who can help validate them for me.

Saturday night, I had a dream about a high rise building a shaking and there was also — *NORWAY*
something to do with a subway and I felt like it had something to do with terrorist.

Last night, I dreamed that we were being bombed or something and things were falling — *NAVY*
from the sky and I was running and taking cover to keep the falling debri from hitting *SEALS*
me. The strangest thing when I looked up in the sky there were seals or dolphins *CRASH*
crashing down and next there was a helicopter crashing from the sky.

The next thing I know I'm where these kids are and I know that someone is coming to — *NORWAY*
kill them so I'm trying to get them dressed and out of their beds so I can move them to
another location and fix their beds so the men that are coming will think the kids are
there but in fact be in a different location. In my dream I'm stressing because I couldn't
get the kids moved fast enough.

Love You More,
Rhonda

129

CHAPTER TWENTY-THREE

costa concordia cruises

Sunday, December 18, 2011: I dreamed that several people and I were in a vessel of some sort. I'd estimate that there were a hundred or more people on this vessel. I dreamed that it had a malfunction and was under water. I remember that it was getting very humid and hot. We were losing oxygen and I was starting to have hard time breathing. I could feel the panic starting to take effect. A few minutes later, I went to another place in the vessel where it was cooler and I was able to breathe better. A few minutes later, I started seeing water rising in this vessel and I felt that we were going to die.

On Saturday, January 14, 2012, my husband and I were sitting in the living room and the news came on the TV with a story about the Costa Concordia Cruise ship. I gasped and told my husband, "Wait a minute, I dreamed of this incident!" I ran to get my dream book and had my husband read my dream that had taken place on December 18th. He looked at me and said, "That is amazing, I don't know how you get all this information." I told him that, for whatever reason, God allows me to see glimpses into the future.

12/18/11 SUNDAY

I DREAMED THAT ME AND SEVERAL OTHER PEOPLE WERE IN THIS VESSEL OF SOME TYPE. I DREAMED THAT THIS VESSEL WAS UNDER WATER AND THERE WERE SOME TYPE OF MALFUNCTION W/ THE VESSEL. I REMEMBER THAT WE WERE LOSING OXYGEN IN THE VESSEL AND IT WAS GETTING VERY HUMID, HOT AND I WAS STARTING TO HAVE A HARD TIME BREATHING. I COULD FEEL THE PANIC STARTING TO TAKE EFFECT BECAUSE IT WAS SO HOT AND HARD TO BREATHE. A FEW MINUTES LATER I HAD WENT TO ANOTHER PLACE IN THE VESSEL WHERE IT WAS COOLER AND I WAS ABLE TO BREATHE MORE EASIER. I'M GOING TO SAY THAT THEY WERE HUNDRED OR MORE PEOPLE ON THIS VESSEL. A FEW MINUTES LATER I STARTED SEEING WATER RISING IN THIS VESSEL AND I FELT THAT WE WERE GOING TO DIE.

CHAPTER TWENTY-FOUR

a birthday gift from mother

*J*n April 1, 2008, my mother's birthday, I called my friend Mary Occhino to connect with my mother. Mary told me that my granddaddy was coming through and that he was with my mother. He started talking about pearls and Mary asked me if I understood. I explained that my granddaddy had bought my grandmother real pearls on their fiftieth wedding anniversary and she was buried with them. Mary told me that my granddaddy and grandmother had a lot of love for each other. My mother then came through and told me to have the oil changed in my car because she hears a ticking noise; it might need to have a tune-up. Mary asked my mother why she was talking about the repairs to my car and my mother replied, "I don't want her to get stuck this weekend." Mary then went on to say that my mother wanted me to look up at the moon between nine thirty and ten o'clock that night and to expect a message from her. I was so excited when I got off the phone with Mary, I couldn't wait until night to receive the message from my mom.

Later that night, around 9:25 p.m., I went downstairs and told my husband, "I'm going to watch my mother blow out her birthday candles in heaven." I went out the door and was standing in the front yard, looking up at the sky. It was cloudy and there was no moon or stars anywhere to be found. I kept standing in the front yard and my husband came out to wait with me. He suggested we should turn out the porch light so we could see better, and I knew my husband didn't really believe I would see anything.

All of a sudden, I heard him say, "Rhonda, look in the sky!" and as I turned around there was a huge fireball going straight across the sky. I cried because I knew my mother was right there with me and I was the one who received the birthday gift that night. My husband was in total shock, he couldn't believe what he had just seen. I told him he was meant to see the fireball and that was my mother's way of opening his eyes to show him that there is no death and that our souls live on forever.

Later that night, my husband admitted that the only reason he came outside was because he didn't think I would receive a message from my mother and he knew I would be crushed. He then assured me the incident made a believer out of him. A few minutes later, my daughter and son came home and they were disappointed that they had missed the event. That night, we were so excited about the birthday gift we'd received from my mother. We stayed up until two o'clock in the morning talking about it. To this day, my husband doesn't ever doubt anything I tell him about receiving messages from our loved ones or spirits from the other side.

AFTERWORD

I wrote *Believe in Your Dreams* to help others who may be experiencing the same type dreams and are hesitant to talk about them for fear of public ridicule. As a young girl, I was scared to talk about my premonition dreams, because I knew people would make fun of me or call me crazy.

My book is meant to enlighten people to the idea that there is no death...that life is eternal. And that, after one's physical time here on earth comes to an end, there is life in the hereafter from which we, still here on earth, can and do receive communications.

We receive many messages in our dreams, and I feel it's important to keep a dream journal, being sure to record the date and content of the dream. No matter how weird the dream may seem, record it in your journal. It could be a day, a week, or even longer until you realize the true meaning of your dream.

Not all dreams have specific meanings, but *Believe in Your Dreams* will help others process their dreams effectively.

Each of us receives messages in different ways. I have come to realize that one way I know I'm having (or had) a premonition dream is when I, myself, am playing a vital part in the dream.

The messages I have received in my dreams are warnings of future events, communications from spirits, angels, friends, and loved ones from the other side. I have also picked up on past life experiences through my dreams.

Whatever dreams may come your way, take care not to discount them, or you may be discounting yourself, your own abilities, and your gift to the world. Let the knowledge you gained from reading this book empower you to embrace your gift.

BIBLIOGRAPHY

Metaphysical Info From:

Begley, Sharon. "Why We Believe in Ghosts, ESP, & Psychic Phenomena." Last modified 2012. http://www.sharonlbegley.com/why-we-believe-in-esp-ghosts-psychic-phenomena.

Medical Info From:

Obringer, Lee Ann. How Stuff Works, "How Dreams Work." Last modified 2008. health.howstuffworks.com.

News information from:

CBS News, "22 Navy Seals dead in Afghan Chopper Crash." Last modified August 6, 2011. www.cbsnews.com.

Ritter, Karl. News & Observer, "Capital Blast." Last modified July 23, 2011. www.newsobserver.com.

Sloan, Kim, and Lisa Hall. Rome News Wire, "Storm cleanup continues after tornado slams Floyd County." Last modified December 27, 2011. www.romenewswire.com.